Environmental Justice in a
Moment of Danger

AMERICAN STUDIES NOW:
CRITICAL HISTORIES OF THE PRESENT

Edited by Lisa Duggan and Curtis Marez

Much of the most exciting contemporary work in American Studies refuses the distinction between politics and culture, focusing on historical cultures of power and protest on the one hand, or the political meanings and consequences of cultural practices, on the other. American Studies Now offers concise, accessible, authoritative, books on significant political debates, personalities, and popular cultural phenomena quickly, while such teachable moments are at the forefront of public consciousness.

Environmental Justice in a
Moment of Danger

Julie Sze

UNIVERSITY OF CALIFORNIA PRESS

The publisher and the University of California Press Foundation gratefully acknowledge the generous support of the Ralph and Shirley Shapiro Endowment Fund in Environmental Studies.

University of California Press
Oakland, California

© 2020 by Julie Sze

Library of Congress Cataloging-in-Publication Data
Names: Sze, Julie, author.
Title: Environmental justice in a moment of danger /
    Julie Sze.
Description: Oakland, California : University of
    California Press, [2020] | Includes bibliographical
    references.
Identifiers: LCCN 2019021691 (print) | LCCN 2019981055
    (ebook) | ISBN 9780520300736 (cloth) |
    ISBN 9780520300743 (paperback) |
    ISBN 9780520971981 (ebook)
Subjects: LCSH: Environmental justice. | Environmental
    justice—United States.
Classification: LCC GE220 .S94 2020 (print) |
    LCC GE220 (ebook) | DDC 363.7—dc23
LC record available at https://lccn.loc.gov/2019021691
LC ebook record available at https://lccn.loc
    .gov/2019981055

Manufactured in the United States of America

28 27 26 25 24 23 22 21 20
10 9 8 7 6 5 4 3 2 1

To friends, compatriots, and colleagues who struggle for justice. To all families coming together and to a better world. But mostly to Sasha, Sofia, and Leo.

CONTENTS

OVERVIEW

INTRODUCTION. ENVIRONMENTAL JUSTICE AT THE CROSSROADS OF DANGER AND FREEDOM

This chapter introduces environmental justice as a social movement and discusses how it has changed over time. Environmental justice advocates conceptualize problems in a particular way that centers their lived experiences and histories.

Social Movements · Anti-immigration · Nationalist Authoritarianism · Climate Change Denial · Structure of Feeling · Freedom Struggles · Ideology and Hegemony

I. THIS MOVEMENT OF MOVEMENTS

This chapter reappraises the histories and theories of environmental racism and the role of Native struggles as fundamental to environmental justice, particularly in Indigenous conceptions of nature and worldviews of human and more-than-human life based on interconnection. It describes the Standing Rock Sioux struggle against the Dakota Access Pipeline, foregrounding activists, scholars, and allies who work on Indigenous land rights and sovereignty claims.

Indigenous Movements · Direct Action · Dakota Access Pipeline (DAPL) · #NoDAPL · Dispossession · Production · Extraction · Militarized and Police Violence · Just Transition · Climate Justice · Indigenous Environmental Network (IEN) · Gender

2. ENVIRONMENTAL JUSTICE ENCOUNTERS

This chapter examines water injustice, slow and fast violence, and environmental racism in Flint, Michigan, and the Central Valley of California. Both are sites of environmental racism, a result of government policy based on neglect and of the concentration of corporate and business power at the expense of democracy and justice.

Radical Democracy · Flint · Central Valley · Deregulation/Privatization · Austerity · Crisis · Invisibility · Water Justice · Human Right to Water · Slow Violence · Storytelling

3. RESTORING ENVIRONMENTAL JUSTICE

This chapter examines environmental and social disasters to illustrate where and how radical hope is generated in dark times, particularly through cultural production. After Hurricanes Katrina and Maria and in Kivalina, Alaska, there are glimmers of how peoples and communities hit hardest by natural and social disaster respond when brutalized by oil extraction, environmental racism, and colonialism.

Disasters · Restorative Environmental Justice · Reparation Ecologies · Anti-capitalism · Solidarity · Climate Justice · Zombie Environmentalism · Climate Debt · Just Recovery

CONCLUSION. AMERICAN OPTIMISM, SKEPTICISM, AND ENVIRONMENTAL JUSTICE

Environmental justice movements challenge the authorities of whiteness, extraction, and violence through diverse voices, media, and perspectives that can be leveraged in powerful ways. They make links, within the United States and across borders, in order to create cultures of solidarity.

Whiteness · Death Cult · Empathy · Radical Hope · Ethics · Love · Solidarity · Optimism · Skepticism

Introduction

Environmental Justice at the Crossroads
of Danger and Freedom

Stevie Wonder's 1975 "Saturn," from the epic *Songs from the Key of Life,* offers a lyrical utopia. Wonder penned the song as an ode to his birthplace (Saginaw), which his collaborator misheard as "Saturn." The song is a loving testament to where Wonder came from and where he wants to go, a vision of a future world much better than the one we inhabit. Unclean air, violence, war, and consumerism are wrapped into an extraterrestrial longing. Four decades later, Wonder's lyrical call is both more urgent and ever distant. In a nation where rapacious corporate capitalism is plundering natural resources, and oil and gas interests fund climate change denial and direct what passes for environmental policy, a world with clean air and without war, rampant consumerism, and extractive capitalism seems nearly impossible to imagine. It is precisely now that imagination and action become essential.

We are living at a precarious moment, with the warmest years ever measured, active assaults on both the disenfranchised and institutions that serve the public interest, and global inequality at its zenith. This moment demands an analysis through the crossroads, an "important structuring metaphor in American Studies," taken from the story that bluesman Robert Johnson cut his deal with the devil down at the crossroads, trading his soul for genius.[1] We are now at a new, yet familiar crossroads and a moment of danger.[2] Neoliberalism idealizes markets, capital, consumer subjectivities, and values over communitarian notions of belonging or justice. We have lived (and died) under neoliberalism for decades, but under changing conditions. The valorization of privatization, finance, and the market and the retrenchment of the state and public sectors are both dominant *and* under stress. As one scholar writes, "The present economic crisis is a moment of potential rupture," because prevailing regimes of "power, profit and privilege" are under serious pressure.[3]

Anti-immigrant sentiments, nationalist populist authoritarianism, militarized security discourses, racist policies, regressive gender politics, and climate change denial (or hostility) are linked, whether in the United States, Italy, India, Hungary, the Philippines, Brazil, Israel, or Poland. Awareness of environmental and other injustices, in the form of vibrant global social movements, is also on the rise because of social media. Although the global economic system is ever more integrated under neoliberalism, hostility to immigrants and refugees is high. Economic inequality has reached levels never seen before in any period of human history. The three richest people in the United States (Jeff Bezos, Warren Buffet, and Bill Gates) own as much wealth as the bottom half of the population (160 million people).[4] In 2013, the world's eighty-five richest people had a net worth equal to that of 50 percent of the planet's population (3.5 billion people).[5] In 2017, the wealthiest global 1 percent gained 82 percent of the world's wealth.[6] It was also the third warmest year on record.[7] Interwoven are crises of modernity (including declining faith in technical authority and scientific knowledge), attacks on media institutions, and the winding down of the American century (albeit with bellicose American exceptionalism denying its demise though red hats and Make America Great Again—MAGA—slogans).

This book begins with an observation: those on the environmental justice front lines have been living, dying, and fighting for a long time. The resurgence of explicit racism is unsurprising for justice activists, who see their lives impacted by legacies of structural domination and racist public policies. Social movements for environmental and climate justice are mobilizing large numbers of people (including virtually) and having a broad national and global impact outside of local contexts. Oil pipeline protests on the Standing Rock Sioux Reservation; responses to mass lead poisonings in Flint, Michigan; mobilizations against police killings of African Americans and other people of color; impassioned actions of Indigenous and small island populations in opposition to climate change—all comprise a snapshot of the hundreds of protests in the United States that have foregrounded the convergence between environmentalism and movements to combat social injustice and inequality. Environmental justice activists make common cause across the globe and mourn the victims of environmental violence and assassination, land defenders like Berta Cáceres in Honduras, Ken Saro-Wiwa in Nigeria, and Chico Mendes in Brazil, who all lost their lives in the struggle against dams and oil and forestry interests. Internationally, extrajudicial killings of those who oppose economic development and deforestation have accelerated, with the death rate rising in the last four years to an average of two activists a week.[8]

The central questions I explore here are based on intensifying social, political, economic, and environmental injustices and responses to these conflicts framed around these questions: What crossroads and moment are we in now? What can we learn from struggles for environmental justice in our moment of danger? My starting point is simple: environmental justice movements—what they are, who is involved, and what they are fighting against and for—help us understand historical and cultural forces and resistance to violence, death, and destruction of lives and bodies through movements, cultures, and stories.

It is precisely in this moment that understanding environmental justice movements is essential. In "Theses on the Philosophy of History," Walter Benjamin writes that to articulate the past does not mean to recognize it "the way it really was," but to "seize hold of a memory as it flashes up at a moment of danger."[9] This book is about the seizing hold of the significance of environmental justice movements. The moment of crisis is the moment of rupture: dominant belief systems and ideologies that dispute them come into view, or sharper relief.

My focus here is on environmental justice movements and the cultures and analytics they advance and embody. These social movements offer important guideposts for troubled times, because they and the people who make them have long-standing political commitments and have done important ideological work grounded in everyday and long-lasting struggles for justice. Starting from the premise that environmental damages are interwoven with political and social conflicts, this book examines how organizers, communities, and movements fight, survive, love, and create in the face of environmental and social violence that challenges the very conditions of life itself.

This book offers a synthesis of environmental justice from a distinctly American Studies perspective, looking at Standing Rock; Flint; Hurricanes Katrina and Maria; Kivalina, Alaska;

and the Central Valley of California. It spotlights how diverse peoples and communities invoke history and justice in facing environmental problems and their roots, in an interdisciplinary and comparative way. Several shifts have made the integration between environmental justice and American Studies obvious. Environmental justice connects race, class, indigeneity, gender, and environmentalism and fundamentally involves social justice. The expanding resonance of the environmental justice movement framework is a concrete response to intensifying and interconnected conditions of pollution and inequality.

Environmental justice scholars and organizers have for well over three decades articulated how race, indigeneity, poverty, and environmental inequality are linked in a toxic brew. Environmental justice is focused on intersectionality (race, class, gender, immigration/refugees, Indigenous land claims/territorial sovereignty) and organized around expanding social and racial justice in environmental terms (land, pollution, health).[10] Contemporary environmental justice struggles in the United States exist within histories of mainstream environmentalism, the civil rights movement, and global resource exploitation inflected through race and racism, colonialism, and xenophobia. After the 1991 "Principles of Environmental Justice," U.S.-based environmental justice movement leaders followed up with the 2002 "Principles of Working Together," guided by the central tenet that "we need each other and we are stronger with each other."[11]

Environmental justice was, and remains, about expansion, connection, and change, governed by this belief in mutuality. That perspective matters now more than ever, as communities face hydra-headed assaults—attacks on immigrants and refugees, rollbacks of LGBTQ and abortion rights, increases in voter suppression and broader retrenchment from the gains of social movements in gender, environmentalism, and civil rights in shaping public policies and discourses. What we call movements matters.[12] Naming problems as environmental racism, inequality, inequity, or injustice has different philosophical and political stakes and distinctly positions the roots and solutions. "Environmental justice" has grown broader and more salient over time, even as what justice means has been vigorously debated by scholars and expanded by activists.[13] The field is ever evolving, but some observations are clear:

> Environmental justice is a compelling umbrella concept. Most versions and visions of environmental justice focus on some component of power and powerlessness, including but not limited to categories of race, class, gender, citizenship/nation-state, indigeneity, and sexuality.
>
> It is easier to recognize the symptoms and examples of environmental injustice, inequality, and racism than to clarify the roots and name the causes.
>
> Environmental justice has evolved to connect closely with climate justice.[14]

The debate and expansion about what environmental justice means is the central point.[15] I use *justice* in a capacious sense, although my notion is drawn particularly from feminist and antiracist accounts. Environmental justice is always already at the crossroads.[16] Rather than fix a meaning in time or space, the process and politics of meaning-making is what makes environmental justice continually relevant. But meaning-making and expansion without a clear sense of politics and position is dangerous. To whit, the U.S. Environmental Protection Agency under President Bush Jr. took away any mention of race and income in environmental justice policy-making to declare that

environmental justice was for everyone, even as federal environmental policy turned ever more squarely in the direction of gas
and oil interests.

Thus, to be clear, my starting premise is that unjust environments are rooted in racism, capitalism, militarism, colonialism,
land theft from Native peoples, and gender violence. The status
quo is too deeply invested in the institutional forces and ideological structures that exacerbate already existing conditions of environmental and social injustice. Tom Goldtooth (Diné/Dakota),
executive director of the Indigenous Environmental Network
(IEN), says, "The system ain't broke. It was built to be this way."[17]

Environmental violence is built into the history of the United
States. It is not an aberration, but part and parcel of a political-
economic system based on racialized extraction of land and
labor, including from Indigenous peoples. Capitalism depends
on control, specifically control of nature.[18] It also relies on the
control and abuse of people of color. Environmental scholar
Malini Ranganathan argues that Flint, where the government
lead-poisoned residents, is not an "American water tragedy."
Rather, government-sanctioned lead poisoning is an example of
racialized dispossession, inextricable from the working of liberalism and processes of "property making and property taking."
Liberalism relies on the "moral primacy of individual freedoms,
especially the freedom to own property."[19] The alienation and
dispossession from the land that settler colonialism demands is
linked to the alienation of African Americans in an economic
and cultural system that political theorist Cedric Robinson calls
"racial capitalism."[20] Historian Patrick Wolfe defines settler
colonialism as a land-centered project with the goal of eliminat-
ing Indigenous societies.[21] Those considered historical property,

and those dispossessed by settler colonialism, cannot enter into a political-economic system based on liberal individualism.

Environmentally just outcomes cannot be expected within existing liberal and capitalist institutions, and they cannot rely on market-based or technology-dependent solutions. Environmental justice activists frame their goals in these terms, especially in their engagement with climate change. Climate justice activists imagine a transition from an oil to a clean-energy economy in a way that does not rely on the market. These activists focus on battling climate change and economic inequality together, with the conviction that "decarbonizing energy and cutting its use in the rich world" can be done in an "egalitarian and exciting way" that does not re-create market logics.[22]

While social movements vary wildly in their politics and approaches, there are recurrent threads and themes. Environmental justice perspectives link justice to freedom and de-link freedom from the market and free enterprise. To do so is to reject what scholars Raj Patel and Jason Moore call Cheap Nature and the cheapening of life. Cheap Nature is the foundational process that enables the cheapening of money, work, care, food, energy, and lives. Environmental justice movements eschew the marketizing and cheapening of life, labor, and land. Justice movements foreground work, care, food, energy, and lives given short shrift in the current global political-economic order.[23]

Climate and environmental justice advocates conceptualize and reframe their problems and center their lived experiences and histories. People of color, particularly African Americans and Indigenous peoples, have been made to live within environmental and bodily risk historically, specifically dispossession and racism.[24] Insurgency and environmental justice as a freedom struggle can reach beyond incorporation into liberal democracy or under settler colonialism. For environmental justice movements, crea-tive, generative, and bottom-up relationships are their raison d'être. So too are history, art, love, and refusal.

Environmental justice is thus a "structure of feeling." Marxist cultural critic Raymond Williams uses this concept to link the social to the personal and to advance a theory of the social that is not just the institutional or formal.[25] Environmental justice as freedom can mean freedom from the violence of histories and systems that structure the present. It can mean freedom from oil and gas and a carbon economy that trades in death and destruc-tion. It can mean freedom to create and reimagine worlds differ-ent from those that are "common sense."

Environmental justice is more than resistance to environ-mental racism and colonialism. It is a set of concepts and living practices that cross time, generations, and space. Freedom is also a capacious set of practices and ways of living in the inter-secting realms of social relations, including those inflected by gender, youth, and sexuality.[26]

FORWARD DREAMING IN MOMENTS OF CRISES

Environmental racism and environmental justice are broad con-cepts, referring to problems that predate the movement's coin-age and organization in the 1980s and 1990s.[27] Environmental justice can mean the social movements, the public policies, and the academic fields. Traditional accounts focus on the general idea that environmental and pollution problems (which often have health consequences) manifest unequally. In policy or soci-ological terms, environmental racism or inequality is an expres-sion of conflicts that distribute environmental risks (exposures) and rewards (amenities) in a socially stratified way (via race and class).

Environmental justice (EJ) was formulated in the United States in response to the articulation of environmental racism (ER) in the 1980s, leading to the "Principles of Environmental Justice" (1991) and President Clinton's executive order on environmental justice (1994).[28] Environmental racism suggests that race and racism are independent factors that influence environmental harms and the differential responses to pollution.[29] Other views of racism and power later gained influence within environmental justice research. In her study of prisons, geographer Ruth Wilson Gilmore defines racism as "the state-sanctioned and extralegal exposure of group-differentiated vulnerability to premature death."[30] Some argue that environmental racism is state-sanctioned violence.[31] Historian Robin Kelley has said in public lectures that "the world is Flint," in that the mass lead poisoning in that city is a direct result of privatization and neoliberalism and its racialized consequences.[32] The ongoing impacts of Hurricane Maria have been understood by activists on- and off-island as not just humanitarian and public health disasters but through a climate injustice/ justice frame, early expression of which was made crystal clear during 2005's Hurricane Katrina.

Using disasters and structural environmental violence as twin frames, this book prioritizes the voices and histories of the environmental justice movement. It is through their perspectives that we can face our present moment with clarity, hope, and principled intensity. Environmental justice is interconnected in the worldview that its advocates advance, focused on intersectionality and power and organized around social and racial justice, whereas polluters and government agencies argue for separation (for example, health as distinct from environmental conditions or housing as unrelated to poverty). In contrast, environmental justice advocates argue precisely for these linkages as commonsense and based on lived historical experiences.

The expansion and transformation of the meanings of environmental justice and environmental racism track American Studies and its shift from its U.S.-centered frame to a more analytically deep and geographically dispersed framework for understanding "America." American Studies, which began in the 1930s, has a fraught history in relation to American exceptionalism—the ideology that the United States is destined to follow "a path of history different from the laws or norms that govern other countries."[33] The field evolved through the 1960s, influenced by liberation movements around race, gender, imperialism, and war. American Studies connects approaches to culture and power, the past and present, and the United States with the world. American Studies and environmental justice are intimately connected to social movements on the ground. Although the field is far more complex, suffice to say that American Studies is defined by the how (interdisciplinarity) and the what (America and American exceptionalism).

American exceptionalism in the post-American century is devastatingly clear in the case of climate change and climate policy, which by definition are issues of justice and disproportionality. With just 5 percent of the world's population, the United States is responsible for 28 percent of the world's excess carbon emissions.[34] Just one hundred companies are responsible for 71 percent of carbon emissions.[35] The United States follows China in terms of absolute emissions but also has double the per capita emissions.[36] Climate justice is also a question of responsibility and morality. President Trump has called climate change a hoax and has signaled that the United States will leave the

Paris Climate Accords, saying the agreement is detrimental to U.S. (business) interests.[37] Yet, U.S. responsibilities go far beyond carbon emissions. American post–World War II technological and corporate culture saw the improvement of nature through technology and increased efficiency as central to the larger political-economic project of development and progress. It has been precisely in this postwar moment, known as the Great Acceleration, in which extreme and sudden spikes in pollution and environmental harm have come into being.[38]

Marxist philosopher Antonio Gramsci's famous motto—Pessimism of the Intellect, Optimism of the Will—structures my teaching, outlook, and indeed this book. The intellect, however, is not just a preserve of the pessimist:

> Too much criticism can feed despair about these "End Times" and can paralyse the will. We surely need an *optimist of the intellect:* theories and concrete studies that map out a more hopeful future, yet ground strategy in realist historical analysis. Perhaps we need to fine-tune our political-intellectual outlook to fit today's chaotic world, where possibilities and catastrophe coexist so intimately.... We need to recover ... "forward dreaming."[39]

Forward dreaming is not based on delusion or naïve innocence but on politics grounded in values. Although to be an optimist is to risk "disappointment and the charge of foolishness," optimism is essential because of the dearth of "hopeful stories about the future" that serve to "express our dreams and desires and correspond to the full range of our experience."[40] Thus the struggle of social movements is, in Robin Kelley's words, to ask and answer: "How do we produce a vision that enables us to see beyond our immediate ordeals? How do we transcend bitterness and cynicism and embrace love, hope, and an all-encompassing dream of freedom, especially in these rough times?"[41]

This book offers environmental justice struggles as a set of cautiously hopeful stories about future and freedom that we need now in rough times, especially when the very notion of future is under great stress due to climate change and assaults on human and social freedom. The optimism *and* the pessimism are that environmental justice movements have been fighting against authoritarianism, extractive industries, rapacious corporate capitalism, white supremacy, and government collusion for a long time. The arguments that environmental justice advocates have been making are gaining visibility and traction outside local communities.

Environmental justice—the analytics and movements—make sense to more and more people who, in less obvious moments, may have settled for an "end of history" or a "colorblind" post-ideological ideology. American studies' tools and approaches, in teaching and scholarship, inform many fields. Gramsci's notion of hegemony is a process in which institutions and historical forces work together to garner consent, and it allows for transformation. Hegemony reveals change over time, showing how what is "common sense" becomes naturalized and is actually a product of institutional and historical influences that are complex and contradictory. Kelley writes:

> It is not enough to imagine a world without oppression (especially since we don't always recognize the variety of forms or modes in which oppression occurs), but [we need] understanding [of] the mechanisms or processes that not only reproduce structural inequality but make them common sense, and render those processes natural or invisible. The Black Radical Imagination is not a thing but a process, the ideas generated from what Gramsci calls a "philosophy of practice." It is about how people in transformative social movements moved/shifted their ideas, rethought inherited categories, tried to locate and overturn blatant, subtle, and invisible modes of domination.[42]

Environmental justice movements, cultures, and worldviews are a counterhegemonic philosophy of practice, a search for freedom beyond local communities fighting bad environmental or regulatory systems. Environmental justice is not (just) about state-centered policy, incorporation, or reformism. It challenges the status quo rather than fixing or tinkering with a system grounded in domination, racial terror, and colonial control.

This book argues that environmental justice movements are freedom struggles. Environmental justice movements have always been about cultures of freedom through imagining and enacting solidarity, radical hope, anti-consumerism and anti-capitalism.[43] Freedom is not an abstraction but is grounded in global and internationalist critiques of imperialism and takes labor, race, class, gender, and sexuality seriously. Many young people are imagining a world different from the one they are inheriting. Populist authoritarianism, militarized security discourses, attachment to racism, regressive gender and sexuality categories and policies, and petrocultures are the preserve of a dying generation of toxic policies and peoples. Those who fear the new world order are the authoritarians who attack climate, economic, and war refugees from Syria, from U.S. wars in Central America, and throughout the world.

Focusing on future and freedom alongside culture, change, and community offers a crucial explanation for the predicament identified by revolutionaries and intellectuals. My (tempered) optimism is structured by experience, analysis using the values of social and environmental justice movements, and everyday interactions with people (especially the very young and elders). I have witnessed the prevailing culture and production of ignorance about environmental injustice and racism change, sometimes in quite marked and sudden ways. For example, broad awareness of Standing Rock and of the lead poisonings in Flint was enabled through social media.

Some changes take longer, but things do sometimes change for the better from a racial and environmental justice perspective, especially one that is intersectional at its roots. In the mid-1990s, the Sierra Club (with other mainstream environmental organizations) was fervently critiqued by communities of color for its demographics and approaches to environmental problems (focused on lawsuits, land trusts, and national-level policy at the expense of local community organizing).[44] Anti-immigration and population-control advocates made eugenic arguments appealing to racist elements within mainstream environmentalism on the logic that more people mean more pollution, and hence, expanding immigration restrictions was good environmental policy. Regressive and racist elements explicitly connected anti-immigration beliefs and environmentalism. These elements sought inroads to take power within the Sierra Club. The anti-immigrant faction lost its attempt to join the board of directors in a bitterly contested election.[45] To fight this effort, a broad coalition emerged with its own vision of interconnection. Over the last two decades, new discussions and alliances took center stage. In 2016 the Sierra Club endorsed the platform of Black Lives Matter, stating that police violence was an environmental issue, a stance unimaginable two decades earlier.[46]

However, despite some changes in the discursive and organizational realms, serious environmental and health problems remain stubbornly high, concentrated among the poor, the politically disenfranchised, and people of color. For example, asthma is an individualized and group disease that constrains lives and life chances. It contributes to overall levels of poor health, high stress, and premature death. Asthma is shaped by factors—political, racial, and spatial—that are both external and internal to bodies and that hit black and Latino children hard. These factors include personal exposures and genetic predispositions, lack of insurance (to manage symptoms), and exposure to air pollution, which shapes landscapes through highways and industrial exposures. Federal health data show that African Americans are 20 percent more likely to have asthma than non-Hispanic whites, and black children still have asthma death rates seven times that of non-Hispanic white children.[47]

Air pollution and asthma are linked to broader struggles against police violence, as I have written elsewhere with colleagues.[48] While Eric Garner was being choked to death by New York City police officers after a "quality-of-life" offense of selling loose cigarettes, he pleaded with the officers: "I can't breathe." Garner, who suffered from asthma, repeated "I can't breathe" eleven times. "I can't breathe" remains a common chant in the Black Lives Matter and ant–police brutality movements. In "Inequality in the Air We Breathe?" journalist Charles Blow writes about environmental contamination and environmental racism in his Louisiana hometown: "Of all the measures of equality we deserve, the right to feel assured and safe when you draw a breath should be paramount."[49] "I can't breathe" thus condenses persistent patterns of pollution and police violence, both of which have denied breath and healthy breathing spaces to low-income communities of color.

"I can't breathe" extends well beyond police violence. It's what journalist Jamal Khashoggi said before his execution by the Saudi government, an oppressive regime based on oil. In Josh Fox's 2017 documentary, *How to Let Go of the World and Love All the Things Climate Can't Change,* Fox says that "pollution is oppressive, it holds you down." In linking environmental racism after Superstorm Sandy in New York City, oil spills in the Amazon, climate change washing away small Pacific islands, and poor air quality in Beijing, the people spotlighted in the film explicitly connect human rights and environmental abuses. Fox suggests that political oppression takes away the freedom and joy that require "deep breath, singing and dancing."[50]

The inability to breathe is a metaphor and material reality of political oppression, state violence, and ongoing legacies of racism. More than two decades ago, I knew a woman, Yolanda Garcia, who was a community leader in the South Bronx. Her son died of an asthma attack and she herself died of a heart attack at fifty-three.[51] Eric Garner's daughter, Erica, died at just twenty-seven, from a heart attack triggered by an asthma episode. The broader reasons are connected to racism and gender discrimination that shape African American maternal mortality (she had just delivered a baby) and structural and partner violence.[52] As Erica Garner said in an interview, "I'm struggling right now with the stress and everything.... This thing, it beats you down. The system beats you down to where you can't win."[53]

This "thing" and the "system" are many-hydra-headed beasts, as African American poet Langston Hughes wrote in his 1938 poem "Kids Who Die." His opening stanza frames whom it's for (the titled "kids who die") and against ("the old and the rich"). The parasitic latter are ravenous, "eating blood and gold."[54]

The things and the system are linked in urban and rural spaces. Extremely high levels of air pollution—some of the highest recorded in the United States—are the everyday norm in tiny, predominantly Latino and Indigenous migrant agricultural communities in California's Central Valley. The land use and economic structure of the Valley render poorer and politically vulnerable residents subject to far greater pollution exposure. The social and environmental conditions of the Valley—highest in the state and sometimes the nation in air pollution, pesticide exposure, water contamination, carceral landscapes, poverty, mortgage foreclosure rates, and low educational attainment—are not accidental but rather structural. This region is particularly vulnerable as the most productive agricultural region in the world and because of its unique geological features: the Valley contains 2 percent of the nation's farmland and 25 percent of its pesticides, 90 percent of which is highly vulnerable to aerial drift.[55]

To invoke Langston Hughes, who gets to live eating blood, gold, and oil, and who is made to die? Racism, capitalism, militarism, colonialism, land theft from Native peoples, and gender violence, in short, culture, history, and politics shape the answers to these questions. Social justice advocates and movements do important ideological work in stripping away status quo power relations. Advocates and movements denaturalize the common sense and in doing so force confrontation with the beasts within that seem ready to devour the many in the service of the few. The tools of American studies are needed to understand the problems we face, in part because of the ideological terrain in which political and revolutionary struggle begins.

Black radical singer and poet Gil Scott-Heron said of his 1970 song "The Revolution Will Not Be Televised" that the revolution was about how

the first change takes place is in your mind. *You have to change your mind before you change the way you live and the way you move....* It will just be something that you see and suddenly you realize that I'm on the wrong page or I'm on the right page but I'm on the wrong note. And I've got to get into sync with everyone else to understand what's going on this country.[56]

Similarly, Robin Kelley writes:

> Progressive social movements do not simply produce statistics and narratives of oppression; rather, the best ones do what great poetry always does: transport us to another place, compel us to re-live horrors and, more importantly, enable us to imagine a new society. We must remember that the conditions and the very existence of social movements enable participants to imagine something different, to realize that things need not always be this way.... Or to put it another way, the most radical art is not protest art but works that take us to another place, envision *a different way of seeing, perhaps a different way of feeling.*[57]

This book is my contribution to understanding singer Marvin Gaye's question, "What's going on?" It offers a primer for those who intuitively understand that environmental racism and environmental injustice exist in far too great measures and who want to make the world less damaged, structured by, and invested in racism, class inequality, gender violence and attacks on immigrants, refugees, and Indigenous rights and land claims. Cultural production, creativity and beauty are necessary to get through the moments of danger we inhabit, the wars without end, the nihilism and violence, and the end of the planet as we know it. Seeking clarity and inspiration from those in the struggle, and having an abiding faith in justice, is what will help motivate people, particularly young people, imagine a world different from the one they are inheriting.

MAKING THE WORLD

This book explores the central tenets of the environmental justice movement in the United States. Each chapter focuses on keywords and case studies. Because the details of every example of environmental justice are important and particular, meriting their own deep understanding, keywords give shape and structure, linking cases and places that are endlessly distinct from one another—Flint, the Central Valley, Hurricanes Katrina and Maria, Kivalina, and Standing Rock. Each is particular and worthy of serious, in-depth analysis of movement organizations, internal power struggles, issue framing, relationships with institutions, and so on. This book positions cases as indelibly connected to one another in the "moments" through which they come into focus. Activists make connections between movements, because their shared analytic allows distinct struggles to target the shared, bigger sources of their problems: capitalism, colonialism, racism. Keywords make it possible to see how threads are interwoven into the fabric of environmental justice struggle. Keywords link the psychic and cultural imaginary of environmental justice movements to provide a counterhegemonic blueprint for survival, resurgence, and solidarity.

To connect is not to collapse or conflate, but rather to highlight relationships and patterns. Sometimes, environmental racism and attacks on land rights and Native lands reflect the attacks on the few by the majority. In the case of fracking, climate change, toxicity, and garbage, environmental violence is perpetrated on the many by the few—by corporations with protection from the state. Oftentimes, "solutions" offered after natural disasters exacerbate and accelerate social and racial injustice, in the form of privatization of schools and housing and destruction of public pensions, what journalist-activist Naomi Klein calls disaster capitalism and social theorist Macarena Gómez-Barris names extractive capitalism.[58] Its antithesis, social ecologies, are those "proposed by artists, activists, movements, submerged theorists, and cultural producers," primarily Indigenous intellectuals, feminists, and activists with anarchist affiliations throughout the "other Americas."[59]

Chapter 1, "This Movement of Movements," a phrase coined by Indigenous activist Dallas Goldtooth (Mdewakanton Dakota/ Diné),[60] lays out the broadest issues in environmental justice as well as the stakes inherent in how environmental justice issues are posed and engaged. The heart of this chapter describes the Standing Rock Sioux opposition to the Dakota Access Pipeline (DAPL), drawing from activists, scholars, and allies who advocate for Indigenous land rights and sovereignty claims. The direct actions at the Standing Rock Sioux Reservation have been a key moment in both climate justice and Indigenous sovereignty movements. The 1,100-mile pipeline is meant to move crude oil near the reservation to southern Illinois, a project of vast scale and scope that has brought significant repression, including threats, prosecution, and physical attacks by the police and military with tear gas, rubber bullets, and guard dogs. The chapter examines dispossession, production, and extraction to understand climate justice, war and militarism, the policing of social movements, and violence. It also explores how solidarity was made through the #NoDAPL movement. Standing Rock is an iconic case of contemporary environmental justice activism that makes Native scholars and activists central and foundational to environmental justice theory and practice, and that shows how Native and non-Native solidarity can be made through struggle.

Chapter 2, "Environmental Justice Encounters," presents two case studies: government-sponsored mass lead poisoning in Flint, Michigan, and air pollution, water contamination, pesticide exposure, and other hazards (natural and social) in the Central Valley of California facing The chapter examines deregulation/privatization, disposability, and hypervisibility/

invisibility. Flint made national and international news in 2015 when the mass lead poisoning of its water supply (and subsequent cover-up) was exposed by doctors, parents, and journalists. Flint is a textbook example of privatization, shaped by decades of race and class conflicts. Childhood lead poisoning and its devastating health impacts on children, particularly those who are low-income and African American, is the story of the failure of government and capital. California's Central Valley faces environmental contamination from different sources and has also been home to vibrant multiracial labor, environmental, and other social movements for almost a century.

Chapter 3, "Restoring Environmental Justice," examines these questions: What is being done to bring us to a more environmentally just United States and world? What is the role of imagination in dark times? It examines Hurricanes Katrina in New Orleans and Maria in Puerto Rico, as well as climate justice efforts in Kivalina, Alaska, using examples of cultural projects that investigate climate disruption, social art documentation projects, and films to highlight anti-capitalism, radical hope, and solidarity. Environmental justice movements are a fertile staging ground for restorative environmental justice, post-carbon and post-capitalist narratives , and the cultures of sustainability and radical democracy that we need now.

The optimism of the intellect is drawn from the knowledge that individuals comprise a loose, confederated environmental justice movement. Many people, particularly elders and youth, have experiences and perspectives that can offer wisdom to those who share values of community and want to protect the the "environment" and "justice," capaciously defined. The optimism I feel is with students and young people, many unhappy with the world that past generations have made and who want to reshape the world with different ways of being and feeling—away from neoliberalism and consumerism, with intersectional justice as its beating heart. They want to bend the arc of justice back into balance to counter a political moment based on death, extraction, violence, domination, and hierarchy.

My intention is to offer a starting point for those interested in particular struggles and to link these together as they have been linked by activists themselves, to spark imagination and hope. What broadens environmental justice to include urban anti-gentrification organizing, water justice, Standing Rock, and just transition/climate justice are a politics and vision, one never dominant in the United States in its role as exemplar of capitalism, violence, and settler colonialism. The vision for environmental justice is one against "eating blood and gold" (and oil)—as in Hughes's "Kids Who Die"—and for making work, care, food, energy, and lives matter, not rendering them cheap, disposable, and dead. This vision echoes the ending of Hughes's poem, in which the joy, laughter, and "song of the life triumphant" rises through the kids who die. Through the first three stanzas, Hughes paints a grim portrait of violence and death against the multiracial kids who die in spaces urban and rural. Thus, the last stanza's hopeful tone is a surprising, yet moving turn. In the poem's breathtaking last lines, Hughes refers to the "life triumphant" through the protagonists. Although they are the objects of violence and death, the "kids who die" bring about the life-affirming emotions of "love, joy, laughter." The turns in the poem are haunting, a testament both to Hughes's clear-eyed realism and his fundamental faith in social change and civil rights.

After seventeen-year-old Trayvon Martin's murder, Hughes's poem circulated on social media as a reminder of police murders of young black men. The lives triumphant in the deaths are the lessons of the environmental justice movement, in the struggles of peoples and communities who are made vulnerable to violence and whose continued survival is a direct challenge to the political and economic order addicted to capitalism, carbon, and white supremacy.

Our triumph is survival, the choices we make and the stories we tell. Sociologist Daniel Aldana Cohen reminds us,

> Every bit of victory is worth winning. That's how I see Antonio Gramsci's "war of position" in the twenty-first century: carbon trench war. From each dug-in position, the chance for a sudden surge forward. We don't know when that moment comes. But we fight stubbornly until it does, so that we're ready. To keep up our spirits, we share stories: about flashes of heroism and about long uncertain living, about liquid dangers and warm pleasures.[61]

This book honors the work of activists who have and continue to be in the struggle, it keeps our spirits up, through the sharing of stories, credit, and support.[62]

Here's to environmental justice activists and believers (may our ranks grow), who sing, breathe, dance, and march in our collective search to make the world not Flint, but Stevie Wonder's Saturn.

ONE

This Movement of Movements

The 2016 address by Robert Warrior (Osage) to the American Studies Association, delivered just after the U.S. presidential election, embodied American Studies scholarship and its relationship to activism.[1] He asked, "Is American studies really a 'home' for Native American studies?" at the precise moment that public knowledge about the standoff at the Standing Rock Sioux Reservation around the Dakota Access Pipeline (DAPL) was at its height. Warrior channeled the concern and anger about DAPL and the election into a cultural expression of solidarity. He ended with a Round Dance to link the audience with Standing Rock in "a big circle of solidarity and hope" that connected "the animate and inanimate, human and nonhuman."[2]

The battles at Standing Rock are exemplary of environmental justice struggles writ large. This observation may seem obvious, but it is not a simple proposition, given the particular Native and tribal issues involved. An estimated fifteen thousand people convened at the Standing Rock Sioux Reservation under the auspices of the #NoDAPL campaign. (The name for the people known as the Sioux is Oceti Sakowin, meaning Seven Council Fires.)[3] Thousands planted their flags and camped in solidarity against the pipeline.[4] Indigenous struggles are at the core of climate change and environmental injustice fights, both against DAPL and in other pipeline struggles. The direct actions at Standing Rock included people from almost three hundred Native nations, the largest such gathering in history.[5] Protesters temporarily blocked the construction of the United States' longest crude oil pipeline. The protests made national news when private security guards set dogs on protestors and the police used water cannons, chemical agents, and rubber bullets.[6] Hundreds were arrested. Policing and violence are central features of the political authoritarianism that attacks indigenous movements with ferocity. In January 2017, one of President Trump's first executive orders expedited completion of DAPL and Keystone XL, another enormous pipeline. The Standing Rock camps were forced to disband in February. And in June, crude oil began pumping from North Dakota's Bakken Formation to Illinois, under the Mississippi River near sacred Lakota sites.[7] Despite DAPL's construction, the fight continues. Activists have traveled or started camps across the United States, against pipeline construction and fracking operations in Nebraska, Iowa, Pennsylvania, Louisiana, Texas, Florida, New Jersey, and Massachusetts.[8]

Standing Rock stands for the Sioux nations and for broader struggles on Native lands against land-based violence. The fight at Standing Rock has great significance in our moment. In the context of (seemingly) ascendant capitalism, militarized violence, and environmental death, #NoDAPL signifies resistance. To argue that it represents environmental justice is to engage with and answer Warrior's question. American Studies is one ideal intellectual, albeit uncomfortable, home for environmental justice. This dynamic, what Warrior calls home/not home, is one that we need to engage with in order to meaningfully enact solidarity between Natives and non-Natives. His invitation to encircle and embody solidarity is a task fraught with meaning, since home is not always a stable ground but can mean displacement, expulsion, or a space of violence and trauma. Solidarity thus depends on understanding history, power, and difference derived from settler colonialism.

Environmental justice and environmental racism are limited yet essential frames for Indigenous land-based social movements. Native activists and Indigenous Studies have had both a foundational and contested relationship to the "people of color" frame that undergirds environmental justice movements. Native peoples and nations are not just people of color facing environmental racism. This distinction stems from their political and historical relationships to the United States vis-à-vis land rights and treaties. For Native peoples in settler colonial nations like the United States, Canada, Australia, South Africa, and Israel, their dispossession from the land is the fundamental starting point for injustice. Native nations must be at the root of serious engagement with environmental justice. As Native environmental justice scholar Elizabeth Hoover writes, "Indigenous communities have a unique stake in the history of environmental racism."[9]

#NoDAPL was primarily a youth- and women-led Native movement. Indigenous youth are at the forefront in climate justice activism. Their activism is focused on connecting the present with the past and future in historically and culturally distinct ways. This chapter reappraises the histories and theories of environmental racism and the role of Native struggles as fundamental to environmental justice, particularly in Indigenous conceptions of nature and of human and more-than-human life based on interconnection. This worldview is radically anti-capitalist. In assessing the significance of Indigenous resistance to pipelines, Julian Brave NoiseCat (Canim Lake Band Tsq'escen) and Anne Spice (Tlingit) write, "Indigenous peoples are more than cameo extras. They are central protagonists in the fight against the forces of capitalist expansion, who would destroy the land and water, and trample indigenous sovereignty, all for the purposes of resource extraction."[10] Indigenous peoples are central in this fight because of their legal status and because large reserves of natural resources are located on Native lands. Native reservations cover 2 percent of the United States, but they may contain about 20 percent of the nation's oil and gas, along with vast coal reserves.[11] Indigenous peoples represent 5 percent of the world's population, but their lands are home to 80 percent of worldwide biodiversity and are rich with natural resources.[12] Thus, Indigenous lands hold economic "value" to outsiders and are prime targets for extraction and top-down economic development.[13]

This chapter provides an overview of Standing Rock, drawing from activists, scholars, and allies who foreground Indigenous land rights and sovereignty claims. The chapter examines dispossession, production, extraction, and violence to understand climate justice, war and militarism, and police violence. Standing Rock and #NoDAPL represent the possibilities and perils of solidarity in a moment of great disruption in the lives and lands of Native peoples. To adapt a question from Indigenous scholar Candis Callison (Tahltan), how does Standing Rock come to matter as an iconic battle for environmental justice?[14]

The pains wrought by the pipelines cannot be separated from Indigenous histories exacerbated and put into sharp relief by the violent response of militarized police in the service of government and capital. Standing Rock also illustrates the psychic and cultural imaginary of environmental justice movements that provides a blueprint for cultural survival, resurgence, and solidarity. It is an Indigenous struggle that generates solidarities between different communities of affiliation, and it is also an Oil War in which policing and violence draw poisonous breath from the War on Terror. Counterhegemony at Standing Rock and beyond is enabled through understanding history and making transformative community through art.

#NoDAPL remains important for the Sioux nations, for Native nations throughout the United States and around the world, and for others who affiliate through solidarity. The protests and communities it created (both actual and virtual) enacted a renewed sense of possibility and purpose, in which media, arts, and cultural associations held special significance. Media, arts, and cultural associations "expand common-sense understandings and inspire a belief in collective agency, if only they have a popular connection."[15] #NoDAPL, like the Chicano movement, Zapatistas, Wobblies, and many others, successfully used the printed word and image in radical and open-ended ways to "imagine a more radical, non capitalist non colonial world."[16]

Another world *is* possible. It existed, however briefly, at Standing Rock.

THE (MANY) PRINCIPLES OF ENVIRONMENTAL JUSTICE MOVEMENTS

In *From the Ground Up: Environmental Racism and the Rise of the Environmental Justice Movement*, lawyer Luke Cole and legal scholar Sheila Foster describe the "tributaries" that laid the foundation for the environmental justice movement: civil rights movements, anti-toxics campaigns, academics, the labor movement, mainstream environmentalists, and Native American struggles. They suggest that these converged to become the river that was the environmental justice movement in the 1980s.[17] Reappraisals of decades of policy change, however, point to major limitations in the efficacy of the environmental justice movement, which are painfully clear in the context of federal environmental policy weighted almost entirely on the side of industry.[18]

To reclaim the radical heart of environmental justice, defanged by two decades of state incorporation and eviscerated at the federal level, I start where Cole and Foster leave off, their "last tributary," the Indigenous Environmental Network (IEN) and transformative politics. The notion of a single environmental justice movement is not accurate now (if indeed it ever was). Environmental justice movements have grown larger, diverse, and global in ways that were not readily visible in the 1980s and 1990s. The notion of Indigenous perspectives as "tributaries" to environmental justice downplays the centrality of these struggles in the United States and globally. NoiseCat and Spice write, "Indigenous worldviews, at Standing Rock, and elsewhere, disrupt the capitalist conception of 'natural resources' that sees 'environment' to be extracted for profit."[19] They echo the argument of political scientist Glen Coulthard (Yellowknives/Weledeh Dene) that "For Our Nations to Live, Capitalism Must Die."[20] Standing Rock is especially significant for the centrality of youth, who called for rejection of patriarchy, sexual violence, and corporate capitalism on what Native peoples call Turtle Island or Mother Earth.

Native perspectives are central to the environmental justice movement, evidenced in the 1991 "Principles of Environmental

Justice." In *Critical Environmental Justice*, sociologist David Pellow argues that the 1991 principles are radical in that they oppose
racism, patriarchy, the excesses of the state and market forces,
speciesism, imperialism, and ecological harm while recognizing
the inherent worth of nonhumans.[21] The principles begin:

> WE, THE PEOPLE OF COLOR, gathered together at this multinational
> People of Color Environmental Leadership Summit, to begin to
> build a national and international movement of all peoples of color
> to fight the destruction and taking of our lands and communities,
> do hereby re-establish our spiritual interdependence to the sacred-
> ness of our Mother Earth; to respect and celebrate each of our cul-
> tures, languages and beliefs about the natural world and our roles
> in healing ourselves; to ensure environmental justice; to promote
> economic alternatives which would contribute to the development
> of environmentally safe livelihoods; and, to secure our political,
> economic and cultural liberation that has been denied for over 500
> years of colonization and oppression, resulting in the poisoning of
> our communities and land and the genocide of our peoples, do
> affirm and adopt these Principles of Environmental Justice.[22]

These principles collectively ask the questions: What and where
is justice for people of color and colonized peoples? What are
the sources of environmental racism and injustice and what can
be done to promote environmental justice? Movement activists
focus on a more capacious timeline than policy-makers and
scholars, arguing that the historical and cultural roots of environmental problems stem from five hundred years of coloniza-
tion and racism.

Environmental justice movements ideologically center agency,
voice, and recognition to reject practices based on exclusion,
hierarchy, and domination. Agency, voice, and recognition of
history are core precepts for a more just future. This belief runs
through environmental justice movement manifestos, which

foreground the notion that "we speak for ourselves" and that the environment is "where we live, work, play."[23] These manifestos demonstrate the worldviews of environmental justice movements: the 1996 "Jemez Principles for Democratic Organizing," the 2002 "Principles of Working Together" and "Principles of the Youth Environmental Justice Movement," the 2002 "Bali Principles of Climate Justice," and the 2008 "Principles of Climate Justice."[24]

The Indigenous Environmental Network was a key player at all the historical gatherings where the various principles were hammered out.[25] IEN is, in the group's words, "an alliance of Indigenous Peoples whose Shared Mission is to Protect the Sacredness of Earth Mother from contamination and exploitation by Respecting and Adhering to Indigenous Knowledge and Natural Law."[26] IEN members have a broad regional and global view of how their problems are linked to global Indigenous struggles. Indigenous communities, their lands, food sources, ways of knowing and being in the world, and bodies—including animals, land, air and water—are at the front lines of pollution and development. Indigenous nations are oftentimes the proverbial canaries in the mine, particularly vulnerable at the first sign of danger that signals the negative health impacts of pollution to other, non-Native peoples.

Environmental justice scholars have traced the environmental, health, and justice implications on Native bodies and communities: Superfund sites and other contamination on Awkesasne land, elevated breast-milk contamination in Arctic Native nations, nuclear dimensions (Native Navajo uranium miners, testing on Shoshone land, and burying of uranium at Yucca Mountain), cross-border (Native/non-Native and U.S./Mexico) air and water pollution, the effects of dam construction, and other consequences. Indigenous worldviews contrast with notions of land, air, and water as environmental resources, or with capitalist and neoliberal notions of ecosystem services based on economistic use value.[27] #NoDAPL is part and parcel of these struggles.

INDIGENOUS/ENVIRONMENTAL POLITICS:
STANDING ROCK IN CONTEXTS

In January 2016, Dakota Access LLC, owned by the Texas company Energy Transfer Partners, announced approval for its application from the North Dakota Public Service Commission to transport 450,000 barrels of oil a day. That amount is more than half of the Bakken oil field's daily crude oil production.[28] DAPL transports hydraulically fractured (fracked) crude oil from North Dakota to pipelines in Illinois. Fracking is a highly contentious method of oil production because of higher risks of earthquakes, in addition to oil spills and water contamination.[29]

DAPL was originally planned upriver from the predominantly white city of Bismarck, but the route was revised to pass upstream of the Standing Rock Sioux Reservation, crossing Lake Oahe, tributaries of Lake Sakakawea, the Missouri River twice, and the Mississippi River once.[30] Initially, the U.S. Army Corps of Engineers approved DAPL without a comprehensive environmental review, drawing opposition from three federal agencies, the Standing Rock Sioux, and other tribes.[31] Lake Oahe is the Standing Rock Sioux Reservation's water supply.[32] Because of public attention and political pressure, on December 4, 2016, the Army Corps of Engineers announced that it would not approve a permit for the pipeline to run beneath Lake Oahe (reversed by President Trump's executive order after the inauguration), but it was built and opened in early 2017.[33] The legal fights continue, even as oil flows through the pipeline.[34]

Many concepts are critical to understanding DAPL and #NoDAPL. These include capitalism, the doctrine of discovery, Indian Wars, Manifest Destiny, neoliberalism, repatriation, and sovereignty, as identified in the #Standing Rock Syllabus, compiled by Indigenous scholars and non-Native allies. Dispossession, production/extraction, and violence are useful starting points for understanding environmental justice at Standing Rock.[35]

DISPOSSESSION AND HISTORICAL MEMORY

What does dispossession mean at Standing Rock? As NoiseCat and Spice explain,

> The fight against the Dakota Access Pipeline is part of a centuries-long indigenous struggle against dispossession and capitalist expansionism.... As indigenous people put their bodies on the line to resist the Dakota Access Pipeline, they are fighting for their sovereignty while offering an alternative relationship to land, water, and each other."[36]

Scholar-activists Jaskiran Dhillon and Nick Estes (Lower Brule Sioux) situate DAPL as an extension of nineteenth-century Indian Wars.[37]

DAPL and #NoDAPL are a conflict over territorial sovereignty and the settler colonial imperative to further dispossess Native peoples, on lands for which they have historical claims and treaty rights. Dhillon and Estes recount the histories of the region beginning from the 1803 Louisiana Purchase, through the nineteenth century, up to the 1970s and the present.[38] After the buffalo were slaughtered, and the white settlers and miners came en masse, the United States turned to legislation to further Indigenous dispossession. Congress passed the Indian Appropriations Act of 1876, which abolished treaty-making, and the Black Hills Act of 1877, which illegally ceded the Black Hills and created the present-day reservation system.[39] Further, in 1890, South and North Dakota exacerbated anti-Indian sentiment in order to break up and open reservation lands for expanded settlement.[40] Federal troops intervened to protect white property and killed military and political leaders such as Crazy Horse and Sitting Bull, as well as more than two hundred mostly unarmed women, children, and elders at Wounded Knee in the Pine Ridge Indian Reservation. Wounded Knee remains the largest mass shooting in the United States. In the early 1900s, Missouri River basin states began to usurp Native water rights for large-scale irrigation projects, and they built a dam system that flooded Native lands.

However, in 1908, the U.S. Supreme Court held that tribes maintained access and control of water within original treaty territory, even if that territory was diminished (known as the Winters Doctrine). The Oceti Sakowin possessed the prior claim to both the river and its shorelines, as spelled out in the Fort Laramie Treaties. Despite these legally recognized claims, the Flood Control Act of 1944 (also known as the Pick-Sloan Plan) authorized the Army Corps of Engineers and Bureau of Reclamation to erect five dams on the main stem of the river, which targeted and disproportionately destroyed Native lands and lives, and four of which flooded the lands of the Oceti Sakowin. Inundation forced more than a thousand Native families to relocate in violation of treaties and without their consent. The Army Corps of Engineers claimed sole jurisdiction over the river and its shoreline. In 1980, the Supreme Court ruled that the United States was wrong in breaking the terms of the Fort Laramie

Treaty of 1868. The court awarded eight Sioux tribes $106 million in compensation. They have refused to accept the settlement, because they want their land returned (as of 2011, the accounts were valued at $1 billion).[41]

The region has also been a central site of Indigenous resurgence and resistance to the U.S. settler state.[42] Estes recounts the 1973 American Indian Movement (AIM) occupation at Wounded Knee in the Pine Ridge Indian Reservation. The occupation was the catalyst for a mass gathering at Standing Rock in 1974, which resulted in the founding of the International Indian Treaty Council. More than ninety Native nations from around the world built the foundations of what would become four decades of work at the United Nations and the basis for the 2007 Declaration on the Rights of Indigenous Peoples.[43]

STANDING ROCK AS ENVIRONMENTAL JUSTICE

Standing Rock aligns with environmental justice movement framing around siting or moving polluting facilities to poorer, nonwhite, and politically weaker communities. The environmental justice movement began organizing in response to the realities that poor communities, often with more people of color, are particularly vulnerable to polluting facilities. Jan Hasselman of Earthjustice and lead attorney for the Standing Rock Sioux says, "Environmental justice is at the heart of this issue, and it's at the heart of our litigation."[44] Civil rights icon and politician Rev. Jesse Jackson joined DAPL protesters in North Dakota, calling the pipeline reroute "the ripest case of environmental racism I've seen in a long time."[45]

In April 2016, LaDonna Brave Bull Allard (Standing Rock Sioux) cofounded the Sacred Stone Camp on her land and invited people to defend it through direct action.[46] The Sacred Stone Camp zine announced the formation of a group of tribal citizens of the Standing Rock Lakota Nation and ally Lakota, Nakota, and Dakota citizens under the group name Chante tin'sa kinanzi Po! (People, Stand with a Strong Heart!). Their mission statement quotes Chief Sitting Bull: "They claim this mother of ours, the Earth, for their own use, and fence their neighbors away from her, and deface her with their buildings and their refuse." It continues:

> His way of life is our way of life—standing in opposition to the Dakota Access Pipeline is our duty.... The Dakota Access threatens everything from farming and drinking water to entire ecosystems, wildlife and food sources surrounding the Missouri. The nesting of bald eagles and piping plovers as well as the quality of wild rice and medicinal plants like sweet grass are just a few of the species at stake here. We ask that everyone stands with us against this threat to our health, our culture, and our sovereignty. We ask that everyone who live on or near the Missouri River and its tributaries, everyone who farms or ranches in the local area, and everyone who cares about clean air and clean drinking water stand with us against the Dakota Access Pipeline![47]

Lakota, Nakota, and Dakota conceptions of way of life includes health, culture, and sovereignty. There is no separation between the land and what happened and happens in and on it. Elizabeth Hoover, in her study of Akwesasne activism against toxics contamination, explains how interconnection works materially. Industrial environmental contamination, histories of settler colonialism, and food are linked because "rural and Indigenous communities often rely on the immediate environment as their main source of food."[48] Interconnection is also linked to Indigenous origin stories, worldviews, bodies, and practices.

Flooding represents a destruction of sacred sites and burial grounds not just to the Sioux, but also the Arikara, the Mandan, and the Northern Cheyenne.[49] The Standing Rock Sioux sued the Army Corps of Engineers in July 2016, charging that the Corps violated the Clean Water Act, the National Historic Preservation Act, and the National Environmental Policy Act. More than 380 archeological sites face desecration along the DAPL route. As Allard explains, the pipeline was going to be next to where her son is buried.[50] She says:

> I was a young girl when the floods came and desecrated our burial sites and Sundance grounds. Our people are in that water.
> This river holds the story of my entire life....
> Look north and east now, toward the construction sites where they plan to drill under the Missouri River any day now, and you can see the old Sundance grounds, burial grounds, and Arikara village sites that the pipeline would destroy. Below the cliffs you can see the remnants of the place that made our sacred stones.[51]

For Allard, there is no separation between the past and the present, between the living and the dead, and between environment, home, and place. The core precepts of the environmental justice movement that "we speak for ourselves" and the "environment is where we live, work, play, and pray" are violated by DAPL and are central to Standing Rock activism.

Native youth were key to making Standing Rock matter to non-Natives. The first public action came from a group of youth who, in May 2016, ran a five-hundred-mile spiritual relay. They ran from Cannonball, North Dakota, to the Army Corps of Engineers office in Omaha, Nebraska. According to Jasilyn Charger (Cheyenne River Sioux), "I run for every man, woman and child that was, that is, and for those who will come to be.... I run for my life, because I want to live."[52] After the pipeline was approved, the youth followed with a two-thousand-mile run in August 2016 from North Dakota to Washington, D.C., where they rallied on the steps of the Supreme Court.[53] Using school-based presentations, legal challenges,[54] eco hip-hop, and public talks, Indigenous youth highlight their voices emerging from the rural and urban front lines.[55]

MNI WICONI (WATER IS LIFE) AND GENDER/ ENVIRONMENT

Standing Rock can be understood through the phrase Mni Wiconi—Water Is Life. Standing Rock is about a relatively new way to extract oil from the land (hydraulic fracking) for the purpose of profit for oil corporations. Discourses and policies that use the notions of environmental resources and ecosystem services base the environment's worth on utilitarian conceptions of market and exchange value. The conflict between Native peoples and corporations also matter, both historically and in the present.[56]

Indigenous worldviews toward nature are not based on extraction to the point of no repair. The natural world is not seen as a "service" for humans, in part because peoples are part of the landscape. Craig Howe (Lakota), Tyler Young, Edward Valandra (Lakota), and Kim TallBear (Dakota) explain the origins of Mni Wiconi—Water Is Life:

> Mni Sose [the Missouri River] is not a thing that is quantifiable according to possessive logics. Mni Sose is a relative: the Mni Oyate, the Water Nation. She is alive. Nothing owns her. Thus, the popular Lakotayapi assertion "Mni Wiconi"—*water is life* or, more accurately, *water is alive*. You do not sell your relative.[57]

LaDonna Allard says, "We are the river and the river is us."[58] According to poet Layli Long Soldier (Oglala Lakota),

People from around the world, from the Pacific Islands to the Middle East to Europe, called out in the Lakota language, "Mni-Wiconi!" It is this sensibility that is important to the present: water is not a "resource," it's not a "utility," it's not negotiable. Rather, it is sacred.... Without water, there is no life. Simple. True. Resonant, down to our very cells.[59]

Standing Rock was framed explicitly not as a message about environmentalism but framed by Native peoples as *water protectors*. Water protectors stand within a particular historical and cultural tradition, specifically a Lakota prophecy about a black snake that slithers across the land, desecrating sacred sites and poisoning the water before destroying the Earth. DAPL is that black snake. According to Dave Archambault, chairman of the Standing Rock Sioux, "There was a prophecy saying that there is a black snake above ground. And what do we see? We see black highways across the nation. There's also a prophecy that when that black snake goes underground, it's going to be devastating to the Earth."[60]

Native relations to the land are founded on an explicitly gendered relationship. The relationship between the interconnected land and body is central to environmental justice and Native activism. Feminist scholar Traci Voyles suggests that the relationship between environment and gender exists because of social roles and histories of settler colonialism.[61] Joe Amik Syrette (Anishinaabe) says, "The water that comes from Mother Earth is like her blood, which gives life." He continues, "A lot of our teaching is to respect all women," which is connected to the ability to bear children in water. This respect is why "for myself to be here, it's a representation of all of the women in my life. Starting with my ancestors, to my grandmother, my mother, my wife, my sister, my daughters."[62]

According to Jackie Fielder (Lakota/Mandan/Hidatsa), a divestment organizer with Mazaska Talks (Money Talks, which works to defund oil pipelines), women have been the backbone of #NoDAPL: "We are only as strong as our indigenous women, and when they don't feel safe, the whole community is in danger.... Mother Earth is feminine and it's definitely our duty to make that heard and do what we can to bring the elements back into balance."[63]

Several Standing Rock activists highlight the relationship between environmental abuse and domestic violence. According to Siera Siera Begaye (Diné),

> The first time I was given a platform to speak on sexual assault and abuse was at Standing Rock. I was a part of a march called Kik Ta! Wake Up, a project led by Rebecca Nagle and other Native women. It was another step of healing for me, my sisters, and our Nahas-dzáán (Mother Earth). The parallels between the abuse that our Mother Earth goes through and the abuse our Native women go through is heartbreaking. She is our life-giver. She is who we turn to, to pray. Praying, surviving, being with all of our indigenous peoples is a step on our continuous journey to healing.[64]

Analytically and experientially, these activists link how the abuse of the Earth and of women are connected.[65] By linking sexual, reproductive, environmental health, and intergenerational justice, Native women and youth activists build upon Indigenous land-based activism and take it in generative directions.[66]

STANDING ROCK AS VIOLENCE AND POLICING

The violent responses to #NoDAPL and the prosecutions of protestors are emblematic of punishment and policing under the expanding security-settler state. On November 20, 2016, North Dakota police officers used water cannons on hundreds of protesters, sending twenty-six people to hospitals.[67] Police used sponge rounds, beanbag rounds, stinger rounds, tear gas grenades (banned in some states), pepper spray, mace, Tasers, and a sound weapon, and private security forces set dogs on activists. More than three hundred people were injured.[68]

In addition to physical violence, intimidation persisted. State authoritarian tactics included arresting protestors for attempted murder and threatening to prosecute journalists reporting the story.[69] Six Native activists faced federal civil disorder charges that could have led to a maximum fifteen years in prison (they settled, but the longest sentence was almost five years).[70] Hundreds of charges were brought by state prosecutors, some of which remain unresolved in early 2019.[71] A proposed North Dakota bill sought to protect drivers from any legal consequences if they hit, injure, or kill pedestrians who are obstructing traffic. This was one of eighteen state bills proposed after Standing Rock, to criminalize dissent, including bans on face masks, seizing assets of protestors, and expelling students.[72] Energy Transfer Partners filed a suit that claims that Greenpeace and its partners are engaged in a criminal network of fraud and misinformation. The complaint, with references to "wolfpacks of corrupt" environmental organizations, uses the anti-mafia RICO Act and anti-defamation laws to wage a "scorched-earth campaign" against #NoDAPL.[73] Like the animal rights movement and Black Lives Matter (classified as an "identity extremist group"), Indigenous movements are painted as high-security risks in the United States and other nations.[74]

STANDING ROCK AS TRANSFORMATIVE POLITICS AND SOLIDARITIES

Standing Rock represents transformative politics for non-Native allies. Standing Rock became a temporary home for fellow (literal and ideological) travelers who reject the economics, politics, and ideologies of DAPL. Joining the fight at Standing Rock and #NoDAPL solidarity meant offering bodies as a form of material support and as a witness to police and state violence. In September 2016, Black Lives Matter (BLM) issued a statement that there is "no Black liberation without Indigenous Solidarity." The statement reads,

> Environmental racism is not limited to pipelines on Indigenous land because we know that the chemicals used for fracking and the materials used to build pipelines are also used in water containment and sanitation plants in black communities like Flint, Michigan. These same companies that build pipelines are the same companies that build factories that emit carcinogenic chemicals into Black communities.[75]

Struggles for BLM and Standing Rock are linked in their defense against ideologies that refuse, as scholar-writer-artist Leanne Simpson (Michi Saagiig Nishaabeg) writes, "to see indigenous and black people as fully human." This inability to see black people as human, known as anti-blackness, is "intrinsically linked to the genocide, white supremacy, hetero-patriarchy, and colonialism used to maintain the dispossession of indigenous people from our homelands on Turtle Island and to erase our bodies from society."[76]

LaDonna Allard's call to come to Sacred Stone Camp is an example of a transformative call to make a temporary home, whose inhabitants intentionally live their solidarity and community. Journalist-artist Sarain Fox (Anishinaabe) describes the power of embodied solidarity:

> For me, it was one of the first times in my life that I could look around and say, "Oh, this is the living, breathing example of exactly what Indigenous people have been fighting for: the right to be and

live off the land.... You could show up at Standing Rock with nothing, just the shirt on your back, and you would be provided with food and shelter. That's really, really beautiful. *So many people must have felt a longing for a place they maybe never had.*[77]

Robin Kelley, speaking of black freedom movement histories, explains how solidarity is *made:*

Comradeship is not built on some metaphysics of race or some shared experience of oppression. Comrades are *made in struggle,* and they are never numerous and they don't necessarily look like us.... Yes, we're real with real desires and cultures and (contested) beliefs and histories, but we are forced to always remake ourselves in relation to Others, to whiteness, to racism/sexism/homophobia. People of Color is not an identity but a relationship defined by racism, dispossession and imperialism. I'm not saying we're just "people" or making some claim to universalism, but rather we need to recognize that as long as "difference" is structured in dominance, we are not free and we are not "made." Making revolution requires making new identities, and that means new relationships and learning from each other.[78]

Making new identities was central to Standing Rock. According to Lewis Grasshope (Standing Rock Sioux), "You felt the power of this place, the romanticism most people came here to fulfill. A lot of people came to protect Mother Earth, to give their lives selflessly for it. And that's what will happen."[79] That sense of community and optimism, the making of a temporary home in the face of violence and destruction, is why the details of how to live, eat, and shelter became a large part of media and activist accounts of Standing Rock.

However, dominant ideologies—such as racism and charges of cultural appropriation—did not disappear magically. To expect otherwise is naïve.[80] Conflicts over cultural appropriation in the inability to center Native perspectives and empty romanticism were certainly part of Standing Rock.[81] Regardless, moments of transformation and solidarity are worth recounting. Palestinian youth and Indigenous leaders from Ecuador came to Standing Rock. Thousands of military veterans convened.[82] Solidarity actions and events continued throughout the summer and fall of 2016, including hundreds on November 15, when activists in three hundred cities around the world participated in a #NoDAPL Day of Action.

TRANSNATIONAL VISIONS FOR A JUST TRANSITION

The ideological visions offered at Standing Rock are among the most important legacies of #NoDAPL. Transformative politics, nonviolent direction action, and the solidarities—however fraught and temporary—offer a vision counterposed against the extractive one embodied by DAPL.[83] The visions and actions at Standing Rock answer, both explicitly and implicitly, the question often leveled at social justice movements: what are you fighting *for*?

Standing Rock activism was explicitly multinational, against transnational oil and gas corporations. It was the Lakota nation standing up for Indigenous rights worldwide. Standing Rock lies on the front lines of a climate justice movement, one that seeks to "Keep it (oil, coal and gas) in the ground."[84] The Indigenous Environmental Network is a key player in the Keep It in the Ground coalition as a component of its environmental justice, just transition, and climate justice organizing.[85] *Just transition* means moving to a "lower carbon economy that recognizes the trade-offs between ... competing needs and priorities (such as energy poverty in the developing world) and seeks to address them in an equitable manner."[86] The central idea of a just transition is that a lower-carbon future takes politics and justice seriously, including (but not limited to) energy access, historical patterns of development, and violence.[87] Environmental justice organizations have been at the forefront of just transition theorizing, legal actions, and policy-making.[88]

IEN's "Indigenous Principles of Just Transition" are worth highlighting. Developed around the same time as the protests at Standing Rock, the twenty-five principles detail the Indigenous values essential to the just transition, climate, and environmental justice movements. The opening principle reads,

> A Just Transition affirms the need for restoring indigenous life ways of responsibility and respect to the sacred Creation Principles and Natural Laws of Mother Earth and Father Sky, to live in peace with each other and to ensure harmony with nature, the Circle of Life, and within all Creation.[89]

This is an Indigenous-led vision, one that many non-Natives can connect to as intuitively powerful in defending worlds and worldviews that are under active and vicious attack.

MAKING ART, MAKING COMMUNITY

Six weeks after the Dakota Access and Keystone XL pipelines resumed construction, the Whitney Museum held an event called "Words for Water." It was a gathering of Native women artists (Natalie Diaz, Heid Erdrich, Louise Erdrich, Jennifer Elise Foerster, Joy Harjo, Toni Jensen, Deborah A. Miranda, Laura Ortman, and Layli Long Soldier) who presented written and musical pieces in honor of the land, water, and people working to protect them.[90] During moments of heightened violence, as well as intergenerational trauma, including the physical destruction of cultures, languages, ways of life, and land itself, art is a indispensable feature of creative sustenance and renewal. Sarain Fox describes the vitality of the arts and how art was made and distributed at Standing Rock, including the Art Action camp.[91] Many examples can be found online and are part of a long tradition of environmental justice art and activism. For example, Justseeds, a collective of artists that makes and distributes images for social movement purposes, created and widely distributed important visual work focused on anti-extraction and anti-pipeline imagery.[92]

Standing Rock matters because of how activists made meaning there and continue to connect their struggles together. Genova Ariel (Mexica) lays out the stakes in terms of connection and solidarities for urban youth of color:

> A win here [at Standing Rock] will set a strong foundation for BLM [Black Lives Matter], [against] gentrification, and anti-deportation struggles in America.... Youth [from Chicago] represented strong at the front lines and continue to support the movement at the No Line 3 Makwa Initiative in Minnesota, against uranium mining at the Wind Caves in South Dakota, and the Keystone XL pipeline in ND.[93]

The structural ties between climate justice, gentrification, and solidarities between communities that seem different from one another (urban/rural, African American/Native) are made by activists who draw connections for outsiders or others who see things in terms of single issues.

The connections circle back to Robert Warrior's question of home/not home and the relationship of American Studies to Indigenous Studies. What is home? To whom? What can be done about displacement and destruction? Who is displacing whom—why and how? Is gentrification similar to and/or different from pipeline struggles or climate change? For poor people and people of color, their precarity threatens their ability to continue to live in the places they made home after historical traumas such as post-Reconstruction and Jim Crow in the South, the destruction of countries due to U.S. foreign policy (Southeast Asia or Central America), or economic development (Operation Bootstrap in Puerto Rico).

This problem is an important one, especially as gentrification in cities like New York, Los Angeles, Oakland, Boston, and San Francisco accelerates and contributes to displacement and widening economic inequalities. In Sunset Park, Brooklyn, real-estate developers took over what was historically known as the Bush Terminal, a group of seven massive buildings on the waterfront that was the iconic site of a Brooklyn industrial development. The new developers called it Jamestown (colonial ironies unremarked) and partnered with other investors to buy a controlling interest in the site from the previous owners, who had defaulted in the wake of the severe damage from Superstorm Sandy.[94]

The community group UPROSE objects to the corporate developers' plans on gentrification grounds. UPROSE has developed a community-based climate resiliency plan grounded in social, ethical, and nonextractive relationships.[95] Environmental justice for UPROSE takes climate, capitalism, and racial justice seriously and together.[96] UPROSE is at the forefront of culture, education, and activism around climate justice, anti-gentrification, and just transition struggles, most recently as host of a Climate Justice Youth Summit, billed as "the largest gathering of young people of color discussing the future of climate change in the country."[97] Hundreds of young people watched a "Culture Not

Consumption" fashion show that received national attention. They ran discussion groups tracing out the linkages between policing, climate refugees, and gentrification. They connected youth justice movements, which bring together issues seen as separate but that the youth activists argue are fused through existing political and economic institutions that devalue the lives of the poor, people of color and young people around the world.[98]

What are the impacts and continuing legacies of Standing Rock? #NoDAPL's successes can be understood in the realm of counterhegemonic ideologies, specifically in community transformation, just transition, and solidarities. According to Matika Wilbur (Swinomish and Tulalip),

> Standing Rock lit a fire in so many of us. Maybe it was because we finally got the opportunity to tangibly feel an entirely indigenous reality. Camp did that for us. And when we left, we were able to take that feeling back into our communities and plant seeds of hope for a better future.[99]

Naelyn Pike (Chiricahua Apache/San Carlos Apache) said,

> We are fighting the invisible, and that is *greed and power*. In this time of chaos, it will be the youth who will give us energy to carry the fight and the wisdom given to us by our ancestors that will hold us to our roots. This is only the beginning.

LaDonna Allard, who started Sacred Stone Camp, echoes Wilbur and Pike: "That's where I have difficulty with things. People say, 'oh, the movement's over.' But it's still my home. I'm not going anywhere. I'm still fighting. I'm only done when that pipeline is dug out of that ground. I've only just begun." And IEN's Dallas Goldtooth explains,

Standing Rock is not only a milestone on the road toward indigenous rights, recognition, and self-determination, it is a beacon for all our collective struggles in this country that are engaging in resistance. It inspired us to stand up to protect our communities, to not falter in the face of militarized police brutality, to reject the status quo of white supremacy, and to continue to build this *movement of movements*.

The Black Lives Matter statement of solidarity reminds us of the significance of #NoDAPL as a "movement of movements." It reads: "Water protectors who are protesting DAPL are engaged in a crucial fight against big oil for our collective human rights.... This is a fight for all of us and we must stand with our family at Standing Rock."[100] BLM urges us to see how the fight to stop pipelines at Standing Rock is tied to the lead-contaminated pipes in Flint, Michigan. The victims of greed and power in the United States are not just Indigenous and black communities, but the agents of greed and power are particularly merciless when it comes to those bodies at risk. And everyone suffers as a result, as we see in the next chapter on water injustice.

TWO

Environmental Justice Encounters

Why should there be hunger and privation in any
land, in any city, at any table when we have the
resources and the scientific know-how to provide all
humankind with the basic necessities of life?

Martin Luther King Jr.

Flint, Michigan, made national and international news in 2015
when government-facilitated lead poisoning of residents through
the city water supply was exposed by doctors, scientists, and
parents. Lead exposure causes major physiological and neuro-
logical damage, with broad impacts on individuals and communities.[1] Government officials knowingly lied after the unelected
emergency manager demanded that the city's water be drawn
from the Flint River, contaminated from decades of industrial
pollution. The water corroded pipes and lead flowed as a result.
Thousands of Flint residents, in 2019, a full four years after the
crisis broke, still face foreclosure for nonpayment of water bills
for lead-contaminated water. What happened in Flint was
both singular and not unique. For more than a century, lead
poisoning has devastated low-income and particularly African

American children, who suffer from disproportionate exposures and unequal protection from the state. Lead poisoning is the story of the intentional failure of government in service of industry. What happened was a double punch of privation and predation. Privation is the act of depriving or taking away the necessities of life. Predation is theft, plundering, or predatory behavior.

Thousands of miles away lies another landscape. California's Central Valley is the most productive industrial agricultural region in the world. It is particularly vulnerable to pollution, with 2 percent of the nation's farmland and 25 percent of its pesticides. Ninety percent of the pesticides are vulnerable to drift, when the chemicals move off the fields, with disastrous health consequences for farm labor, their families, and local communities. An estimated 160,000 residents in the Valley do not have regular access to clean water. The Valley has some of the highest rates of air pollution in the nation, poisoned groundwater, overconcentration of prisons, high rates of poverty and residential foreclosure rates, and low educational attainment.

Flint and the Central Valley are related, although they are quite different (the former is urban and majority African American; the latter very rural, with many Mexicans, Mexican Americans, and Central Americans). The encounters between the Central Valley and Flint are manyfold.[2] After the mass lead poisoning was exposed, Flint residents were given bottled water for household uses such as bathing and cooking. In the Valley, contaminated tap water contains high levels of nitrates from harmful fertilizers, megadairy cow manure, and dibromochloropropane, a pesticide banned in 1977.[3] A subset of Valley residents permanently purchase all their water for household use, a devastatingly high financial burden on a poor populace (up to 10 percent of household income).[4] One article called Central Valley "the Flint of California," although one could also argue that Flint is the Central Valley of Michigan.[5]

Historian Andrew Highsmith suggests that "America is a thousand Flints."[6] What does that mean? Both Flint and the Central Valley are sites of environmental racism, a result of government policy based on active neglect and of concentration of corporate and business power at the expense of democracy or justice.[7] In *Flint Fights Back,* political scientist Benjamin Pauli distinguishes between formal and institutional representative democracy and a grassroots, more radical democratic vision. Lead poisoning in Flint was a result of a direct attack on representative democracy, to which Flint residents and organizations responded with a radical democratic vision. Activists sought "to introduce democracy where it had never existed, to defend it, or to make it more real."[8] This chapter argues that both Flint and the Central Valley are sites of environmental racism, while at the same time they are linked by a collective resistance to neoliberalism and the politics of privatization, privation, and predation. Social theorists Stuart Hall, Doreen Massey, and Michael Rustin describe the hero of neoliberalism as the free possessive individual engaging with others through market transactions. Neoliberalism's ideological project is, they write, "a reassertion of capital's historical imperative to profit through financialization, globalization and yet further commodification."[9] Neoliberalism's principal policy levers are deregulation (reducing the power of government to regulate business) and privatization (private companies doing work in return for public resources, or the selling off of public assets to private companies).

Environmental justice activists argue that pollution exposure, toxic contamination, and environmental destruction are not accidental, but embedded into systems that devalue some lives over others, whether by race, class, immigration status, or some other measure of difference and hierarchy. Activists thus categorically reject the politics of marketization. Deregulation/ privatization, disposability, and invisibility work together for environmental racism to thrive. This chapter examines how premature death, through lead poisoning in particular and toxic exposures in general, is woven into the economic and literal landscapes of the postindustrial city and the agricultural "factories in the field."[10] Pollution and the marginalization of place combine to actively create conditions of premature death for racially marked and politically disenfranchised peoples and places. The expansion of privatization and deregulation and the erosion of formal democracy enable the expansion of capital to control discursive and material landscapes. The workings of, in sociologist Jill Harrison's words, "raw power" shift the burden of pollution to the bodies of the most vulnerable.[11] Racialized and already vulnerable residents are made to bear the risk of environmental violence.[12] Postwar U.S. racialized space limits the life chances and economic security of some, to the benefit of others, in the areas of wealth accumulation and housing through mortgage discrimination and redlining by banks.

Water justice activists foreground a radical democratic view of water *against* neoliberalism and what literary scholar Rob Nixon calls slow violence. Slow violence is "a violence that is neither spectacular nor instantaneous, but rather incremental and accretive, its calamitous repercussions playing out across a range of temporal scale."[13] It contrasts with explosive and spectacular— or fast—violence, such as the militarized standoff at Standing Rock or repressive responses by the state to uprisings and protests of violent African American and other deaths at the hands of police.[14] Anthropologist Chloe Ahmann writes, "Slow violence [is] primed for interpretive debate, even new imaginings of accountability.... Protracted harm can at times condition apathy. [However] it can also inspire *manipulations* of time and creative rearrangements of history."[15] In contrast to the slow violence in Flint and Central Valley over time, the mass lead poisoning in Flint is a media "event," with an identifiable agent of the environmental crime. These inspirations, encounters, manipulations, and creative rearrangements of history in Flint and the Central Valley are multifold. Linked through lead, water contamination, and (slow and fast) violence, social movements stage encounters that are critically and historically aligned around water justice and the human right to water.

Tribal, cultural, and justice conceptualizations of water—as a source of life, a gift, and a human right[16]—are diametrically opposed to a privatized water market defined by consumer shut-offs and punishment for inability to pay.[17] Water is not a condition of property and/or wealth, and access to it should not be framed by debt or citizenship. In 2012, California became the first U.S. state to legally declare that every human being has the right to "safe, clean, affordable, and accessible water adequate for human consumption, cooking and sanitary purposes."[18] Water justice advocates frame water as a human and community need, rather than a natural resource to be extracted, sold, or shut off (when bills go unpaid). What are the stakes in constructing water against neoliberalism? What happens when we connect water pollution with other forms of contamination? Lead poisoning and toxic exposures are unfettered expressions of raw power in a neoliberal landscape. Water has transformed from a source of life to a product that, in its worst iteration, leads to premature death.

Within these conditions of invisibility (Central Valley), hypervisibility (Flint) and premature death (both), social movements contribute counterhegemonic discourses for sustaining life, art, and community. Storytelling is a frequently undertaken by community members and justice advocates. Often poorly understood and much maligned, storytelling is seen as an emotional or unempirical, subjective (and weak) approach versus the muscular truth of data and science. But storytelling is a key component of environmental justice activism because it foregrounds narratives and experiences.[19] Social movements in Flint and the Central Valley advance a radical democratic vision that reaches beyond formal and institutional democracy. They potentially provide a road map for global struggles for justice in the face of catastrophic impacts of drought exacerbated by climate change.

PRIVATION, PREDATION, AND LEAD POISONING

What happened in Flint, Michigan? Simply put, the timeline included austerity, emergency management, state cover-up of environmental and health data, further delays of information, and public-relations stunts (elected officials drinking lead-tainted water). All the while, residents reported "rashes, hair loss, vision loss" and were treated with contempt along with doctors, scientists, and whistle-blower regulators, who were also "dismissed, impugned, and rebuked by state and local authorities."[20]

How and why did Flint's lead poisoning come about in the way it did? Since 1967, Flint had been buying clean water from the Detroit Water and Sewerage Department (DWSD) as a wholesale customer. Flint was cut off from this source of water to simultaneously save and make money (through the newly formed Karegnondi Water Authority, or KWA, which sought to build a pipeline to bring water from Lake Huron).[21] Thousands of Flint residents, including vulnerable children, were exposed to high levels of lead and told everything was fine by agencies that were supposed to protect their environment and health. Each of the following crucial elements merit description: the emergency manager laws, the history of industrial contamination of the Flint River, the contempt directed at the city of Flint by the state of Michigan, the deception by state and local agencies, and the vitriol directed at the "irrational" and "hysterical" public.[22] What frames these factors is encapsulated in these words from the head of Oakland County, a primarily wealthier and whiter suburban county near Detroit, in advance of the emergency manager system: "What we are going to do is turn Detroit into an Indian Reservation where we herd all the Indians into the city, build a fence and then throw in the blankets and corn."[23] The comparisons are clear: African Americans, like their Native brethren, are incapable of civilization. They need to be rounded up, enclosed and treated like animals. Broken places and people of color go hand in hand.

The cross-racial comparison of African Americans and Native Americans is surprising only in its explicit articulation of racist ideologies of anti-blackness and settler colonialism. This cross-racial comparison can also be mobilized from a historical, tribal, and social justice perspective. Kyle Mays, a black/Saginaw Anishinaabe scholar argues that "the #FlintWater Crisis is not just a Black issue, but also a Native issue."[24] Dylan Miner (Wiisaakodewinini/Métis) recounts the Indigenous history of Flint in which he describes how "Indigenous people used riverways, lakes, and trails as a way to travel" using what is known as the Saginaw Trail. Miner describes the 1807 Treaty of

Detroit, which set the template for the next century, specifically
for both the erosion of tribal access to traditional land and out-
right land theft.[25]

In comparing #NoDAPL and Flint, scholars Christopher Petrella and Ameer Loggins ask. "What is the color of democracy?
Who is presumed to be capable of self-governance? And which
types of communities have the right to avoid public health and
increased vulnerability to premature death?"[26] Cross-cultural
and cross-racial connections become part of the repertoire of
resistance and the making of solidarity. Mays writes,

> Indigenous people from Detroit went to Flint. Artists like SouFy and
> Sacramento Knoxx, both Anishinaabe and from southwest Detroit,
> made protest songs to bring awareness to the #FlintWaterCrisis.
> They also donated water and supplies to the residents of Flint. At the
> #HipHop4Flint block party and filter give-away … SouFy stated,
> "all this water here ain from the people that's supposed to be helping
> us, ain from the people who messed up the problem in the first place;
> it's from people that are from different collectives and organizations
> throughout the country. It's not the government. But that's why we
> here, #HipHop4Flint, to do it our own way."[27]

In understanding that justice *comes out of* solidarity, Flint and
#NoDAPL activists are threading their struggles together.

STATE, CAPITAL, AND CRISIS

Artists who focus on "doing it their own way" are responding to
policy choices that have systematically decimated their communities, especially black neighborhoods throughout the urban
United States, from Flint and Detroit to New Orleans, Baltimore, and beyond. Historians have documented how federal
urban renewal policy and highway development, redlining by

banks, and discrimination in government programs (e.g., the GI Bill) converged to produce suburbs and to facilitate white inter-generational household wealth, while actively subverting black homeownership and wealth accumulation. This racial and spatial history plays itself out in the present. Geographer Jamie Peck outlines how states and governments responded to the 2008 financial crisis (precipitated by risk-taking by financial firms) with "austerity urbanism," characterized by deficit politics and devolved risk. These "scorched earth policies" led to a "*financial crisis* [that] has been transformed into a *state crisis* and now that state crisis is being transformed into an *urban crisis*."[28] The outcome in the form of Flint's lead poisoning is thus an effective illustration of privatization, deregulation, and austerity and these forces' actual impact on cities, communities, and bodies.

Flint is an iconic industrial city, emblematic of the fortunes of U.S. industrial power in the mid-twentieth century. It was home to General Motors (whose CEO famously said in 1952, "What was good for our country was good for General Motors, and vice versa") and site of a major sit-down labor strike against GM that ushered in the golden age of organized labor. Despite the strength of unions, specifically the United Auto Workers, there were major environmental costs, which "unspooled over the next half century."[29] Industrial poisoning, with lead as one of many toxins, has thus been central to Flint for eighty years.[30]

Flint is a demographically shrinking city whose population has declined by more than half from 1960 to today, in large part due to the decline of the American auto industry.[31] Flint is now a majority African American city, with 57 percent black and 38 percent white populations. By 2016, it was more than 40 percent poor, one of the highest poverty rates in the country.[32] Government policies and institutions such as banks and charitable

foundations created and maintained racial and economic inequalities through spatial segregation/redlining and deindustrialization of the city in favor of the growth of the suburban
region.[33] Suburbanizing majority white counties surrounding
Flint and Detroit gained financial resources and political attention. GM was responsible for half of the Flint's annual water
consumption but received heavily discounted rates far lower
than residential water users. This tiered rate subsidized corporate large-scale users and was unique compared to other major
cities where all users (residential and corporate) purchased
water at the same rates.[34] These histories are why Flint still has
the highest water bills of any large U.S. water system, even after
the lead-poisoning debacle.[35] Structural and historical factors
make the payment of water bills a nearly impossible burden,
particularly for poor people. More than 17,000 Detroiters and
8,000 Flint residents have faced shutoff and/or foreclosure bills
related to nonpayment for lead-poisoned water.[36]

ANTI-DEMOCRACY AND WATER POLITICS

What does democracy have to do with Flint? The lead poisoning is a direct result of the emergency manager (EM) system,
which became law in 2011.[37] The emergency manager is by definition insulated from formal representative democracy.[38] The
Michigan Civil Rights Commission documented the racial disparities of the EM system.[39] As sociologist David Fasenfest
argues, the EM system is a neoliberal response to fiscal "crisis"
and is anti-democratic because the decision-maker (the EM) is
appointed by the governor and unaccountable to voters.[40] Emergency management displaced democratic institutions, marginalized citizen participation. and weakened civil society. Accord-

ing to Fasenfest, "A city made vulnerable as a result of structural racism was made even more vulnerable through Emergency Management and fiscal austerity."[41]

What cities were put under emergency management and why? Cities subject to emergency management suffered for many reasons, including historical mismanagement by officials and "severe structural economic and social problems." These included ballot initiatives that created legislation restricting the ability of local governments to capture tax revenues from increases in property taxes and extreme population loss due to deindustrialization.[42] Reduced revenue sharing from the state was sudden and drastic, a 33 percent drop between 2006 and 2012. Thus "the State of Michigan helped create the very financial distress in Flint and other cities that it then used to justify the need for Emergency Managers."[43]

The cities under emergency management were majority black and portrayed as broken and lacking fiscal discipline.[44] One scholar writes, "The insertion of an EM appears to be the antidote to perceived (Black) mismanagement, in which the (White) state steps in, replacing old, corrupt, inefficient structures (including union contracts) with new, efficient, sometimes market-driven structures."[45] From August 2012 to October 2013, Emergency Manager Ed Kurtz championed Flint's switch from Detroit water to the Flint River.[46] Because the water was not properly treated, pipes corroded, leaching lead into households. The Michigan Department of Environmental Quality used flawed sampling techniques, manipulated test results, and refused to respond to complaints, whether from regular residents or experts at the U.S. Environmental Protection Agency.[47] In April 2013, the Detroit Water and Sewerage Department offered Flint a substantial reduction in wholesale water rates. The EM rejected the offer and

Flint's joining of the new Karegnondi Water Authority pipeline
was announced in May 2013. Construction of the KWA pipeline
began in June 2013. A year later, nine feet of water transmission
pipe, used to connect Flint to Detroit's water pipeline, was sold to
Genesee County for $3.9 million (Flint later leased back that con-
duit that it had previously owned after it was ordered to reconnect
to Detroit water). The collusion and deception continued even
after the KWA pipeline approval.[48] Flint residents drank unprop-
erly treated, lead-poisoned water for many months. Only after the
crisis exploded into public view were (some) Flint residents given
bottled water to drink until April 2018, when the water program
ceased operation (even though the lead pipes were not yet completely fixed).[49]

The particular sequence of events in Flint are disturbing and
criminal, but they are not unique.[50] In California's Central Valley, hundreds of unincorporated communities have been
"mapped out of democracy," in legal scholar Michelle Anderson's words.[51] The agricultural regions in the Valley, particularly in its southern reaches, import water hundreds of miles
from the water-rich parts of Northern California. Clean water
from the north bypasses poor, farmworker communities through
the California Aqueduct. The water that does exist in the Valley
is often heavily polluted by agriculture.

Legal scholar Camille Pannu argues that anti-democracy
defines water politics in the Central Valley. One example is the
Valley's quasi-public water governance districts. These include
irrigation, reclamation, and improvement districts, which outpace
the number of public water districts. While these districts techni-
cally allow electoral participation, they limit voting rights to individuals (not residents) who own title to land within the district's
area of focus. Most districts determine votes in relation to the

value of a landowner's property: the larger a person's property holdings (in acres) or the greater the value of the holding, the more votes are allocated to that owner. Those who own more land have more political power, and those who do not own land (or who own small plots) are ineligible to vote.[52] Water governance is heavily tilted toward industrial agriculture interests and Southern California cities. In this context, local groups and networks, such as the Community Water Center based in Visalia, work to transform these conditions, institutions, and political structures through organizing, formal representation on water boards, and foregrounding the interests and voices of those not normally part of the water governance system, particularly low-income agricultural, labor, and local communities.[53]

PIPING AND PRIVATIZATION AS POISON

In historian Christopher Sellers's account "Piping as Poison," he documents the long history of Flint's lead poisoning.[54] The ubiquity of lead poisoning is a result of the lead industry and its century-long campaign first *for* its products (like paint) and then, with landlords and other business interests, *against* regulation and mandatory cleanup, despite broad scientific, environmental, and public health consensus about the health impacts of lead poisoning, particularly for children. In 2012, more that 250,000 children nationally still suffered from lead poisoning, despite major gains in lead reduction (lead was taken out of gasoline and paint in the latter half of the twentieth century, but it still enters the environment from insecticides, smelting, and fabricating processes). The problems are heartbreaking in their impacts on individuals and whole communities. African Americans and renters are often the most vulnerable.

There has also been a rich history of fighting against environmentally influenced diseases through community-based activism. During the 1960s and in the context of the civil rights movement, activism around childhood lead poisoning by health
groups and radical organizations was prominent. Groups like the
Harlem Park Neighborhood Organization in Baltimore, the
Young Lords, and the Black Panthers directly took on their communities' higher rates of lead poisoning and lack of garbage col-
lection. They pushed and some responded. Public health advocates and doctors conducted important research, wrote reports,
and sounded clarion calls about the problems of low-level lead
exposure.[55]

Other scholars followed. Nathan Hare developed the concept
of "black ecology" in 1970, in which he suggests that "the concept
of ecology in American life is potentially of momentous rele-
vance to the ultimate liberation of black people." He draws connections between the built environment and black health outcomes and argues that the problems of the urban "ghetto"
constitute an ecological crisis. According to Hare, the black
urban ecological crisis requires a fundamental change in economics as well as a spatial analysis. He concludes that black ecology challenges "the very foundations of American society" and
that "the real solution to the environmental crisis is the decolonization of the black race."[56]

LIVES, KNOWLEDGE, AND BODIES MATTER(S)

Whatever it is called—black ecology, environmental justice, or
community-based common sense—Flint residents knew the
very instant that the water switched to the Flint River that
something was wrong. Sociologist Zoe Hammer writes, "This

knowledge was real and visceral, flowing from the color, smell, taste and detrimental effects of the water on exposed skin."[57] Flint residents were at first ignored, then lied to by the agencies charged with protecting their health and environment. As one mother described, "We were going into city council meetings and being told we were liars, we were stupid."[58]

Public agencies eventually (and reluctantly) tested the water. By August 2014, *E. coli* bacteria results led to boil-water advisories. In October 2014, General Motors announced it would stop using Flint River water due to corrosion concerns. Even the governor's executive staff, which had pushed hard for privatization and the emergency manager system, called for a switch back to Detroit water. In February 2015, the U.S. Environmental Protection Agency (EPA) notified the Michigan Department of Environmental Quality (DEQ) of high levels of lead in the home of Lee-Anne Walters, who had repeatedly contacted the EPA with concerns for her children's health (her water had lead levels nearly seven times greater than the EPA limit).[59]

Yet even then, Flint residents were still not told the full story. Meanwhile, those working in state agencies were provided with bottled water to drink for their safety. DEQ rigged water test results to hide high levels of lead.[60] The story did not truly explode onto the national stage until August 2015, when environmental scientist Marc Edwards released his first set of findings showing elevated lead levels in Flint. A month later, local pediatrician Dr. Mona Hanna-Attisha presented the findings of her analysis, reporting that the proportion of children with elevated blood lead levels had doubled since the switch to the Flint River.[61] Only in October 2015 did Flint stop using the Flint River for drinking water and change back to using Detroit's water system, as the story hit the national and international news.

Until scientific and health testing revealed what Flint residents already knew, locals were actively ignored. Cultural and theoretical lenses (to complement sociological and geographical ones) can help explain why. Water is both "matter" (or material) and "metaphor" (meaning). Some lives—whiter and wealthier—"matter" more and deserve more protection than those (poorer and black) exposed and made vulnerable. Water regulation/deregulation and privatization always "violently racializes."[62] Environmental risk and representation are already racialized, because some voices and bodies and knowledges matter while others don't.[63] For some, the horrors of the Flint lead poisoning were the public exposure and rupture of the "normalized" legacies of race and racism on the bodies of people of color. What was unusual was only the ways in which lead poisoning was made visible and sudden, rather than invisible and endemic.

To those denied access to clean water in the Central Valley as a normalized condition of life, Flint was completely understandable, even expected. It is "normal," even if it is not "right." In the Valley, water and other pollution and contamination happens because water injustice is literally and ideologically built into the political-economic system (which means that unincorporated communities have no water system by design). Not one water justice activist in the Valley would be surprised, for instance, to learn what Art Reyes, an organizer with the Center for Popular Democracy, found in Michigan. Reyes documented that 95 percent of the Spanish-speaking community in Flint did not know about the lead in the water (some heard it from relatives overseas when the lead poisoning hit the international news). Spanish-speaking residents in Flint were also wary of the bottled water program, fearing deportation or immigration enforcement entrapment.[64]

For water justice activists, mainstream discourses of "concern" can be frustrating, a viewpoint that ignores how history shapes policy and environmental violence. But concern can also become a strategic lever for structural change, insofar as it dovetails with activists' own organizing for a more radical democratic vision. This vision is not exclusively based on property, capital, and ownership but on expansive notions of environmental justice and radical democracy. In these historical and ideological contexts, storytelling holds particular political meaning in making voices that are supposed to not matter at all be heard, believed, and seen.

RADICAL DEMOCRACY, STORYTELLING, AND ENVIRONMENTAL JUSTICE

Social movement actors use the connection between polluted places and populations to combat a stigmatizing feature of degradation. Population and pollution in unjust environments are tightly wound together as a result of politics (racism, migration, capitalism, militarism, colonialism, land theft, and gender violence) and history, not biology. This rejection of stigmatization and the claiming of particular places as a "home," despite clear evidence of their extreme pollution, is a driving force for environmental justice activism.

What is home in the context of water injustice and environmental racism? Environmental scientists Carolina Balazs and Isha Ray developed the Drinking Water Disparities Framework. They focus on a case study of Alpaugh and Tooleville, small agricultural towns in the Central Valley with important histories as labor camps, now seen as marginal and "nonviable." They quote a resident who is asked, "Why don't you move" away from the water contamination? That person answered, "Why would you want me to move? That's my house, that's my town, I was born and raised there. Do you think by moving its going to get solved?"[65] This sense of home and belonging is what similarly motivates many Flint residents to stay in their city, despite the lead poisoning and political neglect. Some communities exposed to risk and pollution seek relocation, as in the case of African American communities adjacent to oil refineries or Indigenous villages flooded due to climate change. However, many communities frame their demands for cleanup as pollution reduction or mitigation in their home. They do so through public policy (e.g., responding to environmental impact statements and commenting at public hearings), through the law, and also, significantly, through storytelling.

Stories and how they are told matter. Storytelling is a deeply political act that brings a radical democratic vision to an issue often seen as largely scientific, based in engineering or the realm of policy-making. Community stories "contribute to undermining the legitimacy of state officials and their policies and to shifting public consciousness around the human right to water." Storytelling is a communal and ideological performance that involves both the telling and the act of listening. It "counters individualism and internalization" so that people's individual experiences are transformed into a collective narrative.[66]

Take, for instance, the family and migration story of Susana De Anda, codirector of the Community Water Center in Visalia, California. De Anda details her family's journey from Mexico to California and her own journey to the field of environmental advocacy. She explains that, for her, environmentalism was connected to "my uncles, all farm workers, with leathered skin.... I realized that the yellow planes that flew over us at recess were spraying poison." The body, for the farm laborer, becomes a toxic site. As an organizer for the Rural Poverty Water Project at the Center on Race, Poverty, and the Environment, De Anda traveled to low-income, unincorporated communities where she and her codirector, Laurel Firestone, "saw horrific evidence of the health consequences of drinking water with high concentrations of nitrates, arsenic and other toxins." They began organizing leaders, the majority of them women, to start La Asociación de Gente Unida por el Agua (AGUA), a coalition of communities and nonprofits. De Anda says, "Families who had buried too many stillborn infants and who drove long distances to purchase bottled water they could ill afford rather than drink black tap water that smelled like sewage were galvanized into action."[67]

The Community Water Center is not alone in its fight and its use of storytelling. Sociologist Tracy Perkins's Voices from the Valley is a public, online campus/community collaborative research and outreach project that highlights the photos and narratives of female environmental justice activists in the region.[68] Water, its pollution, and the health impacts on vulnerable populations are one major theme. One photo of the gleaming California Aqueduct and the caption explaining the paradox of water pollution in small farmworker communities is a stark visual reminder of "raw power." Another photo shows Sandra Meraz purchasing water. She led the fight to get a new water system for her community. Meraz, Native American and Latina, was the first woman of color to have a seat on the Central Valley Water Quality Control Board.[69]

Theatre of the Oppressed (TO) techniques have been a key component of Voices of the Valley. TO is based on Augusto Boal, a Brazilian activist and theater practitioner committed to radical popular education principles. TO techniques are an important tool to promote the involvement of citizens, scientists, and health professional in deconstructing toxic exposures, risk factors, and cumulative stressors that impact communities.[70] TO involves knowing the body, making the body expressive, theater as language (and way of inquiry and knowing), and theater as discourse. While not unique to environmental racism, TO has been used to illustrate pollution exposure and public health.[71] Perkins describes a powerful moment (at a public event for Valley activists) and asks, "What did it mean to the women who saw their lives reenacted on stage or honored through photographs in a gallery space? What might everyone else have learned from being witness to their struggles?"[72] When Teresa De Anda spoke, recounting a pesticide poisoning event in Earlimart, a powerful moment was created. She described the incident almost clinically.[73] TO physical reenactment of this poisoning then created a visceral response and an intense, communal painful experience. More than two hundred people in the audience gasped, sobbed, and felt the poisoning in a way that her oral recounting alone did not trigger.

What stories about water and justice are being told in Flint and how? Storytelling is strategic. It widens the circle in the story of the "us," the "how," and the "now."[74] Previously marginalized voices gain center stage. Archives of published material, broadcasted films, recorded reports, statements, conversations, and events, and participant observations about organizing efforts reveal how activists created spaces to share and connect their experiences and stories about water.

In Flint, justice activists centered "the voices and experiences of people whose knowledge has not mattered."[75] "Flint Healing Stories" was a series of events beginning in 2014 in which residents recounted their relationship to water. Because residents were painted as "incompetent, corrupt, and incapable of self-governance," personal stories were "central to efforts to build and expand networks of solidarity, identify and process shared trauma, forge a sense of collective identity, and work collaboratively toward political transformation."[76] At a March 2015 event, Detroit community leaders served as designated listeners for storytellers from Flint. The people on the stage would say in unison, "You have the right to remain silent" before each speaker. The storyteller would then respond, "I waive that right."[77] This dramatic phrase, drawn from courtroom cases, highlighted the ways in which a crime was taking place and silence was a weapon, even though that crime had not yet exploded into public view.

Storytelling included performances and took place through the body itself. In July 2015, activists organized a seventy-mile, eight-day walk from Detroit to Flint, called the Detroit to Flint Water Justice Journey for Clean and Affordable Water. The group walked ten miles a day for one week. What they did was multifold:

> Much of what the Water Justice Journey did—by prioritizing face-to-face conversations, collectively occupying public spaces, and creating venues where everyone's voices and experiences could be heard—was forcefully insist that those lives *did* matter, building relationships and strengthening existing ones to prevent those lives from being discarded. As Detroiter Valerie Jean Blakely said during the first day of the walk: "Everything we do, we are planting seeds for people to feel ready to stand together to ignite something in their heart to say, "Hey, I love my neighbors enough to make sure they have water."[78]

These acts—conversation, physical occupation and bodily movement and motion, and highly participatory venues for voice and experience—make black brown and poor lives and knowledges matter. Storytelling and walking collectively foreground water politics as a space of generation, relationship, and creativity rather than arising from privation, scarcity, and fear.

Flint and Detroit residents organized their own research projects in the face of government neglect and criminal behavior. Like the Flint residents' working with doctors and scientists, community groups in Detroit organized as We the People of Detroit Community Research Collective. In 2016, the project released a collaboratively researched manuscript called *Mapping the Water Crisis: The Dismantling of African-American Neighborhoods in Detroit, Volume One.* The statistical evidence gathered helped set the stage for the unveiling of the Water Is a Human Right Bill in Michigan.[79] Although the legislation did not pass, it remains an active campaign by organizers. This report was followed by the People's Tribunal for Violations of the Human Right to Water, a social justice theater project developed by activists to inform the general public about the mass water shutoffs in Detroit and the criminal negligence that led to the poisoning of Flint's water supply.[80] At the People's Tribunal, the trial proceedings were orchestrated as a moral drama featuring testimony from people who had faced shutoffs and lead exposure through contaminated water.

Such storytelling moments are powerful ruptures in the technoscientific façade of normalized and slow violence. Done with a political stance based on collective power and the democratizing impulses of art, performance, storytelling, and knowledge-making, these collaborations—scientific and artistic—can be incredibly impactful. But in order to feel nonextractive, or to avoid a performance of pain for outsiders, certain principles are paramount. These collaborations must be grounded in environmental justice principles; namely, the idea that "we speak for ourselves." Thus, the dictum of "not using the master's tools to dismantle the master's house" demands a different approach to environmental racism and lead contamination, one with power at its root. Some broke publicly with Marc Edwards, the scientific expert who legitimized early concerns, for many reasons, but at least in part because of his arrogance (he later sued some activists for defamation).[81] As Benjamin Pauli recounts of the dispute, what is at stake is a set of complex questions: "Who decides what deserves to be known? Who gets to speak authoritatively about what is known? Who decides who gets to know what is known? Who produces the knowledges that is known?[82]

Thus, science and art can be *about* a place/community /environmental problem, or it can be *with and by*. This difference (about/with) is not mere semantics. Art *by* Flint residents and art *about* Flint are distinct in terms of who is involved, why, and who is the intended audience. Two high-profile Flint-related art concept pieces illustrate the potential pitfalls in artistic engagement with environmental problems. One, by African American conceptual artist Pope.L, involved signing and selling bottles with Flint River lead-contaminated water.[83] The other is a collaboration between conceptual artist Mel Chin and fashion designer Tracy Reese in which the water bottles given to Flint residents were remade into high-fashion design.[84] In these cases, the artist is from outside Flint, and the audience is primarily art insiders.

Contrast these with the projects of Flint-based artists and art educators.[85] Natasha Thomas-Jackson, Executive Director of Raise it Up!, a youth-centered intersectional arts organization, argues that positionality matters, against an extractive mode.[86] They "use song, poetry, dance, and visual imagery to tie the water crisis in Flint to water struggles all over the globe and to the psychospiritual connection that African and indigenous people have to land and bodies of water."[87] Art, pedagogy, freedom, and liberation are intricately connected.

Flint became a national and international story, then largely disappeared from the mainstream media. Central Valley's water, air, and pesticide pollution remain, as they have for over half a century. Philosophically and pragmatically, both cases raise the questions, who gets to live and who is made to die?

Privation and predation under neoliberalism are the undergirding ideologies that shape the commonsense assumptions of policymakers and corporations. Hegemonic ideologies see the lumpen living in their midst as both essential (farm labor) and/or disposable (auto workers). Capitalism extracts from land and labor, leaving polluted landscapes in its wake. Dehumanization and a distorted "blame the victim" mentality are linked. Social movements, in contrast, focus on fundamentally different sources of politics at their root, based on need, capacity and love, reciprocity, and community.

Flint's resonance extended far beyond Michigan and became a salient symbol. In suggesting that the "World Is Flint," Robin Kelley focuses on the histories and ongoing policies that exacerbate racism, principally neoliberalism and privatization. Environmental injustice and violence "work" because they are embedded in the prevailing economic and political structures that produce some places and bodies as pollutable. David Pellow calls this status "expendability," and this allows the status quo based on racism, profit, extraction, and violence to remain. Environmental justice activists disrupt these conditions through storytelling and the body to reclaim the right—separate from income and debt—to drink and breathe.

The World Is Flint thus can also refer to the possibilities of complex solidarities. In the ways that Black Lives Matter allied with the #NoDAPL movement, the crossings between Indigenous, Chicano, and black communities embody what solidarity looks like across and between highly polluted spaces and across time. Central Valley activists like Sandra Meraz and Susana De Anda and activists in Flint and Detroit de-normalize existing environmental and social conditions of slow and fast violence and pollution. They act to bend power from the raw power of exploitation, environmental and otherwise, into new social and material realities.

Art and activism are key components in that ongoing effort. Sharing stories is a powerful attempt to correct the "flood" of neoliberalism in a world where global warming and water shortages loom large. People's stories, artistic practices, knowledge-making, and coproduction of scientific knowledge are deeply political acts. In these acts, environmental justice activists in Flint and the Central Valley seeks to recenter the lives and voices not meant to matter, indeed, those primed to die, as central protagonists in pitched battles for radical democracy.

THREE

Restoring Environmental Justice

This chapter examines environmental and social disasters to show where and how radical hope is generated in dark times. Music, websites, films, and graphic novels compose a counterhegemonic soundtrack for a restorative environmental justice politics grounded in solidarity. These cultural productions differ in genre, content, and context. What they all share is a belief that culture matters in environmental and social struggle. They critique marketization and consumerism, oil and gas cultures, and at times, gesture to anti-capitalism. To say culture matters is not to move focus away from the state.[1] Resource allocation and regulation matter greatly, especially in the neoliberal context where the U.S. Environmental Protection Agency has effectively dismantled clean air, climate change, and environmental justice programs.[2] Culture is not mere prescription or a road map for policy, but it can spark a fire, especially linked to movements on the ground. Boots Riley, musician and director of *Sorry to Bother You* (a 2018 radical anti-capitalist film), describes how "rebellion is edited out of the worlds we have built. . . .

We put those rebellions back into the stories we create and consume."[3]

Environmental disasters are not new, although they may feel new to those insulated from the impacts of colonialism and racial capitalism. Thus, the responses of the environmental justice movement to environmental disasters illustrate how communities respond from a justice standpoint. In 2005, Hurricane Katrina set the template for how race and class sharpen the negative impacts of environmental disasters, both in disaster planning and in the racialized aftermath of privatized "recovery." After Katrina, research identified how race, toxicity, and rampant wetland destruction and suburban development in the context of privatization and deregulation magnified the already devastating impacts on the backs of the poorest and most vulnerable victims in New Orleans and beyond. Hurricane Maria in 2017 was the most recent devastating illustration of the dangers of our age, with formal state-centered politics closely aligned with oil and gas industries and other corporate interests. Many other hurricanes have involved these same dynamics (Sandy, Florence), but these two are particularly important culturally. Katrina opens the era; Maria mirrors and exemplifies it. For both, justice activists argue that the destruction was shaped strongly by racism, colonialism, and history, in sharp contrast to the neoliberal individualized market view of problems such as natural disasters and their purported solutions.

The urgency of the political moment generates a radical momentum, created and reflected through culture. In both post-Katrina and post-Maria are glimmers of how peoples and communities hit hardest by natural and social disaster respond when brutalized by oil extraction, environmental racism, and colonialism. Environmental justice perspectives are critical in the terrain of consciousness, through restorative environmental justice. Here, I draw from world systems sociologist Jason Moore's "reparations ecologies," examples of which include the food sovereignty and climate justice movements. He defines reparations ecologies as politics that is "fundamental to remembering the violence and inequality of modernity and coming to terms with a way of organizing life—not just between humans, but between humans and the rest of nature—in a way that is emancipatory." Reparations ecologies is "a rethinking of what nature, and humanity, and justice means," insofar as it demands a "taking of key domains of life (education, healthcare, housing) out of the market. What's coming into focus is a politics that is revolutionary in a new way—which questions capitalism's very basis, through especially the nature-society binary."[4] Environmental justice movements have long argued for this rethinking, removing the market and making connections that collapse and exceed binaries and dualisms. This chapter places environmental justice at the center of this revolutionary politics by adding important missing dimensions and histories to reparations ecologies. Specifically, restorative environmental justice widens the scope to centralize Indigenous and black perspectives and, crucially, culture and community.

Restorative environmental justice is an analytic based on environmental justice practices, principles, and worldviews. It draws from restorative justice (criminal justice) and restoration ecology (ecology). In environmental science, the opposite of extraction can be thought of as accretion, accumulation, restoration, or conservation. Restoration ecology is the scientific practice and "process of assisting the recovery of an ecosystem that has been degraded, damaged, or destroyed."[5] Restoration ecology and restorative criminal justice begin with similar premises, although they are vulnerable to the same critiques that they are too individualized and reformist.[6] A few social scientists have raised the links between restorative justice and environmental justice.[7] One area of significant overlap between the two domains (although not named as such) has been in Native environmental sciences, from both Native and non-Native scholars working on Indigenous land stewardship and comanagement issues.[8]

Restorative environmental justice is explicitly decolonial and integrative, including humans as animals and imagining humans and nonhuman nature in a nonextractive modes. Iñupiaq leader Colleen Swan, talking about Kivalina, Alaska (one of hundreds of Indigenous villages in the Arctic that will be destroyed as sea ice melts and rates of coastal erosion increase), illustrates the concept succinctly:

> If we want justice in Kivalina, *restorative justice,* we have to lead. We have to take the lead, because we know what needs to be restored. One of the important things that I see is getting that *self-determination kind of thing* that we used to have a long time ago, to where we never depended on anyone outside the village for anything. Our people have, well I wouldn't say that we lost it, but I would say that it was stolen from us. A lot of things need to be restored.[9]

Critical consciousness and a focus on histories and storytelling are the environmental justice movement's major contribution to fighting during and through this moment of danger. The environmental justice movement links politically disenfranchised peoples and communities across time and space. Social movements imagine different ways of relating—between peoples and between people and the natural world. In a brutalizing era focused on death and resource extraction, characterized by apocalyptic forecasts and emotions such as despair and nihilism, environmental justice movements contribute their cultural imaginaries and share their histories and worldviews.

Environmental justice activists and scholars reject despair as they always have. Their communicative modes are principled resistance, life affirmation (against capital accumulation and economic growth), and solidarities based on radical empathy, humor, grace, and transformation. Rebellion and resistance stories are part and parcel of restorative environmental justice, grounded in *more*. Abundance, life, and affirmation are counterposed against fear, deprivation, and chaos. Anishinaabe cultural theorist Gerald Vizenor's notion of "survivance" articulates how Indigenous struggle involves more than reaction to tragedy. Survivance is "an active sense of presence," continuation, and creativity.[10] According to Indigenous philosopher Kyle Whyte (Potawatomi), collective continuance for Native peoples is the "community's capacity to be adaptive in ways sufficient for the livelihoods of its members to flourish into the future."[11] Native presence is not based simply on the past, but on the past that shapes the present and future in historically and culturally specific ways. Restorative environmental justice thus disrupts dominant modes of engagement with climate change and politics.

Radical visions for art, beauty, practice, and revolution already exist in many places if we look—from Oakland, to New Orleans, Puerto Rico, and throughout the Americas. Theorist Macarena Gómez-Barris describes social ecologies, which "challenge frames of knowledge" that seek to "bury the subtlety and complexity of the life force in the worlds that lie within the extractive zone." These include the body in the realm of the nonhuman world, beyond "mere resistance to the more layered terrain of potential, moving within and beyond the extractive

zone."[12] Environmental justice scholar Giovanna Di Chiro articulates a "living environmentalism" framework that highlights
intersectional, feminist, and global coalition politics forged by
activists in environmental justice and women's rights organizations.[13] Living environmentalism, social ecologies, and restorative environmental justice are radical acts for those whose lives,
labors, and homes are abused and extracted. Sometimes, survival itself is a radical act.

TROUBLING CAPITALISM/CARBON

One of the central contributions of environmental and climate
justice activists is to make clear how the prevailing status quo
targets their lands and bodies. Environmental justice activists
trouble the notion that the capitalism and the carbon-based
economy that drives it are mostly fine. Rather, capitalism and
carbon live out and through systematic dispossession, production, extraction, and disposability—in short, death and violence.
Environmental justice perspectives eschew the market, force a
reckoning with history, and otherwise disrupt American excep-
tionalist, technophilic, and teleological narratives. To do so is to
disrupt the holy grail of capitalism as the natural state of being,
particularly in the United States, and thus begin to answer the
question, what comes next?

The connection between imagination and capitalism is a fundamental component of revolutionary change. In his influential
1979 essay on science fiction writer J.G. Ballard, Marxist literary
critic H. Bruce Franklin observes that because of Ballard's psychological investments in imperialism, white supremacy, and
capitalism, the author is predisposed to "mistaking the end of
capitalism for the end of the world."[14] This observation has been

oft-reworked by cultural critic Fredric Jameson as "It is easier to imagine the end of the world than to imagine the end of capitalism."[15] Franklin's actual question was, "What could Ballard create if he were able to envision the end of capitalism as not the *end,* but the *beginning,* of a human world?"[16] In asking this question, he points to the limits of imagination under late capitalism that are oriented almost entirely toward death and decay.

This provocation—to imagine the end of capitalism as we know it as different from the end of the world—is the starting point here for restorative environmental justice. The question of what is being restored and for whom is a central one for people of color, postcolonial and neocolonial subjects, and Indigenous peoples. To remain hopeful in the face of catastrophic histories, including the end of a way of life, is essential. As environmental scholar Janet Fiskio writes, the dominant affective mode for her students in a privileged liberal arts environmental studies context is of despair and nihilism about the scale and scope of climate change.[17] Thus, affect and emotion related to climate change and cultural destruction are often (unsurprisingly) shaped by lived realities of class, nation, and community.

This observation is not to say that despair is unwarranted. The world is facing hothouse earth (a chain of self-reinforcing changes leading to very large climate warming and sea-level rise), and those with the least culpability are hardest hit (e.g., global climate change refugees such as those from the Pacific Islands and the Caribbean).[18] Several reports from the Intergovernmental Panel on Climate Change (IPCC) have found that global warming is unequivocal, that it is mostly human-caused, and that the impacts are severe. The 2014 documentary *The Wisdom to Survive: Climate Change, Capitalism, and Community* elaborates how the impacts of climate change will be, as what one expert

says, "a crime against humanity." These crimes include intensifying conditions of drought, flooding, and wildfires as well as
water acidification and the wide-scale death of ocean life,
including coral reefs. The human and social impacts are massive, leading to global movement of populations and increased
violence and war. In addition to elaborate detail on the human
consequences of climate change, this film emphasizes the role of
art, beauty, witness, and suffering in the face of pain. These,
suffused with righteous anger, are what characterize climate
justice and restorative environmental justice worldviews and
practices.

Restorative environmental justice is based on praxis, history,
and relationships, and examples abound. One related to climate
justice is Re-Locate Kivalina, a transdisciplinary global collective working with local delegates to initiate a community-led
and culturally specific relocation, using social arts methods and
online media.[19] The project is founded on "solidarity and
engagement" and a long-term dialogue in which a global partners travel to the village on a recurrent basis to develop shared
priorities. As one of the codirectors of the organization says,
"Re-Locate recognizes the roots of structural inequality in
Kivalina's displacement and seeks to frame prospects looking
forward that renegotiate power structures and realize material
change in the village. These material changes and political
retooling efforts are one and the same."[20]

Re-Locate is focused on politics, "beyond recognition, capac-
itating Kivalina's own comprehensive set of actionable strategies
is our goal."[21] Re-Locate is grounded in the limits of recognition, to develop what the group calls "transformational empathy." As the chairman of the Kivalina Relocation Planning Com-
mittee explains, sympathy and empathy are distinct:

We get a lot of sympathy from a lot of people ... but we need more than sympathy, we need empathy.... To empathize with another you've got to really put yourself in their shoes for an extended period of time. Empathy is going to take time ... it's more than feeling sorry for someone. To really empathize with someone in our situation you really have to experience what we experience; eat our food; face our seemingly compounded dilemma. We know that there are solutions to our situation. We know that there are ways that our problem can be resolved.[22]

Kivalina's Colleen Swan explicitly rejects the affective realm of paralyzing despair. Janet Fiskio writes on the "unbearable grief" in teaching on climate change, and she teaches to push against current ideologies of sustainability solutionism, to bear witness and avoid despair. To do so means to work with the students in "causing problems, asking questions, causing *trouble*."[23] Trouble means both difficulty and unrest, and through these dual terms we can understand environmental justice as a cultural and historical analytic. Environmental justice is also embodied as a form of solidarity. Instead of relying solely on conventional or neoliberal forms of combating climate change, new discourses arise out of feelings, opinions, desires, and bodily forms of making solidarity through protest—in other words, imagining a "vocabulary for talking about climate change," which includes mourning, solidarity, hospitality, and love.[24]

Troubles, mourning, hospitality, and love are precisely the modes of engagement that people of color, particularly Native peoples and African Americans, have relied on as generative spaces of hope in the face of ongoing structural death and violence. Life through and after horror have been recurrent features in Native and black stories in the United States since the "original sins" of genocide and slavery. Horrific violence and the return of the repressed are central features in those natural disasters where social and racial inequalities magnify the pain for those hardest hit.

We can see this cultural mode of representation, suffused with satire and humor, in 2018's *Sorry to Bother You*. In it, director and musician Boots Riley rejects individualism as a failed response to the death-oriented political economy under capitalism. Historian Robin Kelley argues that the film "is not a vision of a dystopian future; it is a commentary on five hundred years of human history."[25] This film lightly exaggerates situations that are already ubiquitous, such as debt and precarity, to paint a landscape of racialized economic exploitation. The protagonist, Cash, excellently puts on his "white voice" to sell lifelong labor contracts of the desperate to a company called WorryFree. He battles his conscience, his radical artist girlfriend, and a labor organizer friend. He then discovers a plot by an amoral CEO to secretly (and without consent) turn the company's workers into horse-human hybrids called equi-sapiens, more powerful and profitable as hybrids than humans.

Geographer Aidan Davison describes human practice as the "drawing toward and into ourselves of worldly things: things living and nonliving, artefactual and ecological, human and nonhuman, earthly and heavenly."[26] The equi-sapiens are a dark version of human and corporate practice, a fusion of things living (human bodies) and nonliving, human and nonhuman, earthly and a synthetic hell created out of our culture's desire to engineer (improve?) the natural through the technological for the sake of profit. The film's main character exposes the corporate malfeasance. Rather than leading to WorryFree's demise, the stock soars as this technological miracle streamlines labor costs to maximize efficiency, as if "to emphasize … how the endgame of capitalism is terrifyingly bleak, and how the government (and frankly, consensus public opinion) will forever side with moneymaking conglomerates."[27]

This bleak ending has edges of optimism. Cultural critic Franscesca Royster identifies what she calls a black post-soul eccentricity of musicians and artists. Sound and performance in particular performers are eccentric and slippery; they shift "and make strange the body of the performer . . . to transform the listener's and collective audience's relationship to their bodies," to reclaim imaginative and corporeal freedom from the social death of slavery and legacies of racism. She writes that "eccentric sound" (and in the case of film, images) "flips the switch, splits the tongue. It highlights dissonance in terms of the relationship between body and expected pitch."[28]

Cash, now an equi-sapien, leads his fellow equi-sapiens in knocking on the door of the CEO who made them horrific. The repressed return through revolution: what ensues is arguably a form of rebellion. This sentiment is repeated in the song "The Guillotine" in the film's soundtrack. The song opens, in an insistent and urgent voice, as the last scene of the movie visually ends with Cash and the equi-sapiens. Through its title, its call ("hey you"), and its invocation of "your" war, the song offers a revolutionary challenge against injustice laid bare at "your door."

The film (and soundtrack) is not optimistic in a traditional sense, but rather points to the possibilities of redemption through the horrors and humor. A film invested in reconciliation and sympathy would end with Cash's body intact, a new emotional growth, and a successful romance. But Riley is not interested in individualized redemption. His vision is of rebellion and revolution coming out of community and exploitation.

What justice means in the film is not altogether clear, but at the very least there is a sense of just desserts. That Cash is altered genetically is a crime, but in his solidarity knocking at the door he is arguably freer than when we first encounter him as a passive, precarious worker. Restoring environmental justice is not about a return to a prelapsarian state of nature or of perfect balance. These states of nature and balance have historically been denied to people of color. Rather, restorative environmental justice is a call for solidarity focused on accountability, art, and the continued search for freedom in a body or bodies shaped by the forces of racism, capitalism, and technology.

TROUBLING HURRICANE KATRINA

One of the most important "events" that set the stage for our current moment of danger was Hurricane Katrina. On August 29, 2005, Hurricane Katrina hit the Gulf Coast. It brought massive winds and covered a large landmass, but its true devastation was in the aftermath, when the levees broke, which led to massive flooding. During the first week after the hurricane, 80 percent of New Orleans was submerged, which sent thousands to the Superdome and the Convention Center, last resorts for people who had little means to evacuate the city.[29] Almost two thousand people died, hundreds of thousands were displaced, and there was more than $100 billion in property damage. Race and class were key factors that shaped the failures in evacuation planning and in the storm's aftermath. After the flood, links between development and forced displacement of African Americans have been well documented by social scientists, who talk about "green gentrification" and how disaster planning exacerbated rather than mitigated class and racial inequality.[30]

Even before Katrina, environmental justice activists were anticipating the racially disproportionate effects of climate change—for example, in coastal flooding and the health effects of heat waves—through the Environmental Justice and Climate Change Initiative (EJCC).[31] The EJCC predicted all that unfurled during the hurricane, an analysis that has since been taken up by hundreds of climate justice groups in the United States and around the world.[32] According to a consultant on the Louisiana's evacuation plan, "Little attention was paid to moving out New Orleans's 'low-mobility' population—the elderly, the infirm and the poor without cars or other means of fleeing the city, about 100,000 people" (these were the exact populations stranded in the Superdome in terrible conditions after the levees broke). When explicitly asked at planning meetings about what to do with those populations, "the answer [of government officials and disaster planners] was often silence."[33] The silence of technocrats and disaster planners results from a lack of recognition of extreme social, class, and racial difference.[34]

This silence about powerless people is not surprising from the standpoint of the powerful. In sharp contrast, Ethnic Studies scholar Curtis Marez asks, "How might scholars of American studies and related disciplines approach the problem of disposable people in Katrina's wake?"[35] The answer: through culture in its myriad forms. He cites Johari Jabir's analysis of Mahalia Jackson's performance in the film *Imitation of Life* (1959), specifically her performance of the spiritual "Trouble of the World." Jabir argues that she evokes black New Orleans funeral rites within a broader culture "aggressively indifferent" to African American life and death. This insistence is striking given a broader culture invested in black silence. Jabir writes,

When Mahalia enters the film with her New Orleans dirge interpretation of 'Troubles of the World' … we are reminded that at any
moment, centuries of historically repressed crying, 'weeping and
wailing' buried deep in the souls of black folk, could erupt and consume all the elements … [of] whiteness, wealth, and status.[36]

The moment is always now, and art is the truth about the
complex ""troubles of the world."[37] Troubles in New Orleans
transcend time. To counter the state-sanctioned silence and
environmental racism that preceded and followed Katrina, the
2009 documentary *Trouble the Water* is invaluable as a cultural
text about the hurricane. The tagline for the film is "It's not
about a hurricane. It's about America." But how? The protagonists of the film are Kim Rivers-Roberts and her husband,
among the 100,000 "low-mobility population" left behind during
the hurricane. These people are those unable to leave because
they are too poor, too ill, or too unfree (Kim's brother was
trapped in a jail that flooded and was abandoned by guards).
The film includes twenty minutes of footage that Kim shot during the storm, as well as her journey afterward—literal, bureau-
cratic (struggles with the Federal Emergency Management
Agency, or FEMA), and metaphoric. Kim embodies those
unseen and unheard by bureaucrats and disaster planners before
the storm and in its chaotic aftermath. By focusing on the hurricane through Kim's eyes (through first her video footage and
then her post-Katrina travels and travails), the film centralizes
her troubles, her perspective, and experiences.

Put simply, like Mahalia Jackson, Kim Rivers-Roberts trou-
bles the narratives of American exceptionalism and capitalism.
The threads between Jackson and Rivers-Roberts are multifold.
Their lives as black women are central to their worldview, and

their struggles exemplify more than their individual identities and problems (whether in a funeral dirge or in physically surviving the hurricane and returning to New Orleans). Where they differ is in their musical genres. Rivers-Roberts is a performer-rapper known as Queen Koldmadina, and her song "Amazing" focuses on her pain and strength as two sides of a coin. She narrates her life throughout the film, including gun and state violence and her time in foster care. Her song elaborates her experience, including the death of her beloved mom from AIDS and drug addiction. The song builds to a powerful aural climax, her sonic and personal power complete, in a culture invested in the pain and weakness of the powerless. The message of the song, and the film is simple: *We exist. We live. We survive. We matter.*

Troubles and unfreedom are in part about the dead and the haunted in the wake of legacies of slavery. Black unfreedom and lack of control over their own bodies, both during and after Katrina, were made painfully clear in the racist media representation of "looting." In the immediate aftermath of the hurricane, Rivers-Roberts and other survivors go to the military base that sits on higher ground for protection and relief. They are met with guns of the U.S. military. The National Guard and other militarized responders (some just back from tours of duty in Iraq) overstated the threats of black violence. One account of the hurricane's aftermath noted,

> At the time, fear of looting led to the formation of quasi-militia groups, primarily made up of white residents or local police, who guarded areas in and around New Orleans, leading to racially motivated violence that would take years to prosecute. Encountering dead bodies in the water became common.... If the water was moving fast, they would be forced to tie the body to a permanent object.[38]

The racialized language of violence and the active repression of the histories of race and class that shape these states of unfreedom echo the notion of the "repressed," or what some call zombie or undead environmentalism. Zombies, in their American incarnation, strip Earth back down to its essential parts: mankind, nature, survival. The original zombies emerged when humans were denied control of their own bodies and sought death as an escape. One scholar argues that the zombie has come to serve as the primary symbol of escapism itself—where "the fictional enslavement of some provides a perverse kind of freedom for everyone else."[39] Zombies return. They don't die because the past doesn't die. Violence that is never reckoned with can never be forgotten.

Hurricane Katrina and the return of the dead is a central theme of *Come Hell or High Water.* The 2013 documentary focuses on Derrick Evans, a teacher

> who returns to his native coastal Mississippi when the graves of his ancestors are bulldozed to make way for the sprawling city of Gulfport. Derrick is consumed by the effort to protect Turkey Creek, which his great grandfather's grandfather settled as a former slave. He is on the verge of a breakthrough when Hurricane Katrina strikes the Gulf Coast.[40]

Evans works to restore the river, but he refuses to characterize his work as a "conservation" story.[41] Like the Indigenous water protectors who reject Standing Rock as an "environmental" conflict, Evans's framing of what is being protected and how matters. What makes the story of Turkey Creek a *restorative* environmental justice story is the foregrounding of the violence of history and racialized economic and land-use development. Hurricanes like Katrina and social and economic disasters like top-down economic development and gentrification in black communities are explicitly linked by local residents, particularly those who are being displaced.

Kim Rivers-Roberts connects Hurricane Katrina with past and continuing state violence and the privatization of development in postdisaster "recovery." She focuses on a juvenile detention center built across from a high school and people using the works of local African American artists without permission. Katrina is still "alive and well" for the poor and black.[42] Rivers-Roberts says, "The Lower Ninth Ward didn't get enough help or money to rebuild. That's why so many didn't come back—that's Katrina in another form." She links violence and trauma and retells her story in different forms. Despite government and private development efforts to make New Orleans less poor and less black, she makes her story the centerpiece of trauma *and* creativity.[43] To do so is to expand the affective and emotional terrain of climate change, privatized land use and economic development, and racial terror.[44] Those most vulnerable are least responsible, hence the injustice. But those most vulnerable are also, arguably, the most prepared for the postcarbon, postcapitalist future, in part because they have survived in the face of socially and politically sanctioned death.

This survival in the face of death is what philosopher Jonathan Lear calls radical hope. He renarrates the story of Plenty Coups, the last great chief of the Crow Nation, who said, "When the buffalo went away the hearts of my people fell to the ground … and they could not lift them up again. After this nothing happened." Lear asks, "How ought we to live this possibility of collapse" and vulnerability?[45] Although Lear is not talking about climate change, his questions illustrate contemporary philosophical and ethical dilemmas. How do people maintain the ability to hope and believe in renewal that survives destruction? Indigenous scholars and activists argue, in Nick Estes's words, that Indigenous history is the future. Similarly, Kyle Whyte argues that Indigenous perspectives on climate change situate the present time as "already dystopian," situated through dialogic narratives with descendants and ancestors. Taken together, these writings suggest that discourses on hope, crisis, and survival must take Indigenous histories, presents, and futures seriously to enable solidarities.[46]

HURRICANE MARIA AND JUST TRANSITION

This question of how to maintain hope and believe in renewal in the face of social and environmental violence, death, and destruction is being asked and answered on a daily basis in Puerto Rico. Between September 16 and 30, 2017, Hurricane Maria devastated the Caribbean.[47] Maria has a special infamy in the annals of disaster and environmental racism.[48] More than 3.5 million U.S. citizens, including residents of the U.S. Virgin Islands and Puerto Rico, faced catastrophically slow disaster recovery. Equally disastrous was a fully dysfunctional mainland political climate that dwarfed the FEMA ineptitude after Hurricane Katrina. Six weeks after Hurricane Maria, more than 70 percent of Puerto Rico lacked electricity and running water. Eighty percent of agricultural crops were destroyed. Full power restoration did not occur until August 2018, almost a year later. This blackout in Puerto Rico was the longest in U.S. history.[49] The U.S. government counted the hurricane's death toll at 64. This number was challenged repeatedly, culminating in officials in Puerto Rico accepting the findings of an independent investigation that put the death toll at 2,975 people, nearly fifty times the official

estimate.[50] The President Trump disputed the higher number
and boasted, "We did a fantastic job."[51] Reports directly compared disaster relief after Hurricane Harvey in Texas and Hurricane Maria in Puerto Rico. The disparities are devastating—in
financial resources (helicopters, food and water, tarps), personnel, timeliness of response, and financial relief for victims.[52]

Many historical, political, and technological issues shape the
question of why and how hurricane recovery was disastrously
slow in U.S. territories. One is debt. Hurricane Maria and its
aftermath cannot be separated from the debt and austerity politics that preceded it. The origins of Puerto Rico's $72 billion debt
include mismanagement and the colonial economic system's
sanctioning of predatory "vulture" hedge funds. The Financial
Oversight and Management Board runs the island's economy,
and their determinations cannot be challenged by the Puerto
Rican government. This structure is reminiscent of the anti-
democratic practices in Flint under emergency management.[53]

Rather than accept a discourse that poses austerity as the
answer to a problem of its own creation, those who advocate
debt cancellation connect debt to historical development and
the economic exploitation baked into the history of Puerto
Rico.[54] The struggle against Puerto Rico's debt echoes earlier
debates about debt cancellation and historical carbon debt
(HCD). Climate debt is "a special case of environmental injustice where industrialized countries have over-exploited their
'environmental space' in the past, having to borrow from developing countries in order to accumulate wealth, and accruing
ecological debts as a result of this historic over-consumption."[55]
Rectifying inequality requires countries that have, in the past,
emitted levels of greenhouse gases in excess of an equal per capita allocation to receive less than their equal per capita alloca-

tion in the future. This also works in reverse for countries that have, in the past, emitted levels lower than their equal per capita contribution. Countries with a positive HCD are considered debtors, while those with a negative HCD are considered creditors. Historical carbon debt is a powerful conceptual tool for assigning emissions restrictions and costs to those who have benefited the most from past development.

The reframing of debt is connected conceptually to calls for a "just" recovery, rather than a market-based one. Using the frames of just transition and just power, a coalition of local, community-based organizations in Puerto Rico and on the mainland has called for such a just recovery, one that includes debt relief, transparency in distribution of resources, and attention to environmental justice issues, principles, and policies. These grassroots groups are actively resisting the top-down desire of economic and political elites to literally and socially reshape the island through high-end development, debt bondage, and privatization of public services, including education. Thus, in Puerto Rico as in Flint, social movements are advancing radical and participatory democracy in the face of anti-democratic restructuring. Resistance and organizing are strong in Puerto Rico, even as residents remain traumatized by the hurricane and its aftermath. The debates parallel those post–Hurricane Katrina, in which political and economic elites used the disaster as a pretext to rebuild the education and housing system, advancing privatization and charter school agendas. In response, and in line with environmental justice movements in the United States and around the world, hundreds of organizations and major coalitions that have emerged post-Maria. These groups and networks advance climate and environmental justice frames in their search for solutions post-Maria, including advocating renewable energy and a people's platform.[56]

Puerto Ricans in the diaspora joined with those on-island in creating art for organizing. A number of groups and initiatives popped up in response to state failure post-Maria.[57] Cultural productions show the energies of musicians and artists in centralizing Puerto Rican voices. *Hamilton* creator Lin-Manuel Miranda donated portions of the proceeds from his blockbuster musical and brought together many famous Puerto Rican artists to create a benefit song.[58] In visual culture, artists illustrated their accounts of life after Maria.[59] Graphic artists created two major compilations, *Puerto Rico Strong* and *Ricanstruction,* produced by Edgardo Miranda-Rodriguez. *Ricanstruction* stars La Borinqueña, the Puerto Rican heroine, fighting alongside Batman, Superman, Wonder Woman, and other DC Comics characters.[60]

In Puerto Rico, culture becomes a resource in a context where climate injustice grows as a direct consequence of continuing coloniality, privatization, and policy racism. Justice activists in climate, environmental, and anti-austerity movements struggle to reframe the "official" story of debt and social failure. Rather, justice activists draw upon a longer timeline of history, politics, and movements to combat the state and capital interests that seek to remake the island as a natural and economic resource to be further exploited. In situating their struggles against marketization with those in New Orleans and Flint, justice activists in Puerto Rico add their threads to the counter-hegemonic struggle for restorative environmental justice on an island long defined by its beauty and natural resources to be plumbed, and by bodies in pain.

Violence and trauma kill and create. They disrupt at the same time that they can generate new orders. Some of what is created can seem monstrous, while other responses are utopian. Restoring environmental justice means taking the standpoint of African American and Indigenous lives as the starting point. It means taking fact, fiction, and narrative approaches more broadly in the accounts of why and how we (at many scales) got here and how we might survive. Examples include fictionalized equi-sapiens or solar panels after a devastating hurricane. Restoring environmental justice takes history into culture (and vice versa) and centers life beyond extractive capitalism and its affiliations with carbon and hierarchy.[61]

Radical freedom activists have long known how revolutionary politics is performative and cultural. Benjamin Lay, an eighteenth-century Quaker abolitionist, knew rebellion well. As historian Marcus Rediker recounts,

> He was a dwarf, barely four feet tall, but from his small body came a thunderous voice. God, he intoned, respects all people equally, be they rich or poor, man or woman, white or black. Throwing his overcoat aside, he spoke his prophecy: "Thus shall God shed the blood of those persons who enslave their fellow creatures." He raised the book above his head and plunged the sword through it. As the "blood" [bright red pokeberry juice] gushed down his arm, several members of the congregation swooned. He then splattered it on the heads and bodies of the slave keepers. His message was clear: Anyone who failed to heed his call must expect death—of body and soul. . . . He knew he would be disowned by his beloved community for his performance, but he had made his point. As long as Quakers owned slaves, he would use his body and his words to disrupt their hypocritical routines.[62]

Performative disruption can sway, even if not suddenly. Quakers became staunch abolitionists, in part because of Lay's provocations and challenges to the common sense of his age. Environmental justice activists create a completely different structure of feeling than that proposed by venture capitalists, charter school proponents, and developers. The equi-sapiens, the zombies and dead bodies *are* us and we are them.

What we do, how we treat political and natural others, and how we think matters. When we bother to look, we see things that disturb us. At the same time, we see rebellion all around. We should be troubled by the world, and we should seek to trouble it. Scientists, artists, and thinkers are "staying with" the trouble we live in. Feminist technoscience scholar Donna Haraway writes, "It matters what thoughts think thoughts. It matters what knowledges know knowledges. It matters what relations relate relations. It matters what worlds world worlds. It matters what stories tell stories."[63]

Environmental justice movements write and rewrite stories of freedom under violence and hope after destruction. The question of solidarity is what to do about what troubles us. People seeking to expand freedom have always questioned the common sense of their (and our) day. We cannot look away. Radical and feminist historians of labor and social movements look to spontaneous protests of evictions, to wildcat strikes outside of formal unions, and within and beyond the body. We can see glimpses of solidarities all around us. Some are old, as Rediker writes of Lay's visions: "Against the common sense of the day, when slavery seemed to most people as immutable as the stars in the heavens, Lay imagined a new world in which people would live simply, make their own food and clothes, and respect nature."[64] Restorative environmental justice is one such lens for an optic of freedom and solidarity.

To live beyond terror, to feel joy and radical hope, is to be free—just not WorryFree.

Conclusion

*American Optimism, Skepticism, and
Environmental Justice*

For the earth to survive, capitalism must die.

Scott Alden

I began as an American optimist.... I became an
American Skeptic, not as to the long search for justice
and dignity, which is part of all human history, but in
the light of my nation's leading role in demoralizing and
destabilizing that search, here at home and around the
world. Perhaps just such a passionate skepticism, neither
cynical nor nihilistic, is the ground for continuing.

Adrienne Rich

Hurricanes Katrina and Maria show how existing political and environmental systems perpetuate deep social, spatial, and racial injustices. They are not unique to our moment. Writer Pankaj Mishra argues that "the religion of whiteness becomes a suicide cult." He quotes James Baldwin and W. E. B. Du Bois, who note the deep psychological investment in whiteness that has implicit environmental and spatial dimensions. Baldwin wrote that the rulers of the "higher races," struggling to hold on to what they have stolen from their captives, and unable to look into their mirror, will precipitate a chaos throughout the world which, if it does not bring life on this planet to an end, will bring about a racial war such as the world has never seen.

Whiteness denoted, according to Du Bois, "the ownership of the earth forever and ever." But, Mishra writes, "many descendants of the landlords of the earth find themselves besieged both at home and abroad, their authority as overlords, policemen and interpreters of the globe increasingly challenged."[1]

There is no greater illustration of the suicide cult of the moment than in matters climate or environmental. Thus, the significance of the environmental justice movement is in challenging the authorities of whiteness, extraction, and violence through diverse voices, media, and perspectives. Environmental justice movements make links, within the United States and across borders, and create cultures of solidarity. The links between urban policing and pipeline violence, between oil production/extraction and gentrification, are themselves connected. These lines are not straight—they are jagged. They move between places, groups, and past-present-future. It is in these interconnections that radical justice movements are imagined and made. Art-making and protest are life-affirming in an extractive capitalist context that invites deaths—of nature, peoples, and planet.

American optimism ends the false dreams of American ideologies. Optimism of the intellect and American skepticism mean sharpening the critique and pointing to multiplicities, rather than to a techno-optimist "solution." As Robin Kelley writes,

> Revolt here is the search for meaning, knowing there are no absolutes—including no absolute justice or freedom. [The film] *Sorry to Bother You* chooses revolution over the lone Camusian rebel, suggesting that our survival as a species and as a planet depends on

the overthrow of capitalism, the redistribution of wealth, and a complete reordering of society based on collective needs.[2]

Revolution means engaging with radical hope and a focus on praxis and social movements.[3] Justice and solidarity are when a black worker gleefully cheers on a Latino worker wildcat walkout in an Indianapolis factory.[4] We see them in decolonial food justice movements in Native and Latino communities. We see them in Janelle Monae's Afrofuturist film *Breathe* and Stevie Wonder's soundtrack album *The Secret Life of Plants,* indebted to a nineteenth-century Bengali science-fiction writer, scientist, and polymath named Jagadish Chandra Bose.[5] Wonder "reclaim[s] the green world, its expansiveness and freedom, for black people … in collaboration with human and nonhuman others, open and insistently quare."[6]

Feeling for other beings can lead us away from the death cult of whiteness, carbon addiction, and capitalism. When we feel terror at a barnacle goose chick on its way down a four-hundred-foot sheer cliff, or when we feel sadness when a mother orca won't let go of its dead baby for seventeen days,[7] our empathy for other beings is activated. This empathy has been in far too short supply, embedded as we are in the political and economic systems that structure our lives. Colonialism and slavery left ongoing legacies of economic abstraction that render organized violence normal. Justice movements reject the common sense of capitalism and such abstraction. Kelley writes,

> We die more often at the hands of cops—good cops—than by Nazis and Klansmen. And we die in prisons. And we die by gunfire at the hands of acquaintances, loved ones, and by random acts of violence. And we die slowly from being poor, from lack of health-care, from self-medication, from the water we drink, the food we eat, and the air we breathe.[8]

Environmental justice movements reject the slow deaths and fast violence everywhere. Environmental justice is about living and loving beyond the shadows and the numbers. It is about love and creation in a moment that fetishizes death and spurns care. It is about reclaiming the ethics of morality and widening the circles to respect land and home and to acknowledge trauma and history. We have much more work to do. Welcome to the future . . .

ACKNOWLEDGMENTS

Acknowledgments are hard to start and even harder to write (I've written two before, and they are better—trust me). When does the debt end and appreciation begin? To my father who helped shape much of what is fundamental in my personality? We didn't share many politics, but I miss him a lot. To my mother from whom I learned to be curious? To my family? Probably.

Let's jump forward. My teachers and friends at UC Berkeley in the early 1990s taught me a lot about how to write, think, and struggle (to my students who think California is progressive, read some history). Environmental justice organizers inspired and motivated me then, as now. Without Ethnic Studies and English in my life, I would never have ended up (quite accidentally) in American Studies at NYU. What a place to land—with Andrew Ross at the helm, committed to scholar-activism in myriad forms.

Fast-forward another decade. The University of California is everything that a public institution should be. Coming in as director in the midst of the budget crisis was rough going, but it taught me much about how to be nimble in political-economic crisis. Since becoming founding chair of the American Studies Department at UC Davis, my colleagues have much sustained me. The University of California Press gives out a button at its booth at the American Studies Association that reads "scholar-activist." I'm proud to be connected to UC Press and the American Studies Now series, edited by the formidable Lisa Duggan and Curtis Marez. Niels Hooper was instrumental throughout the process of completing this contribution to the series. David Correia and David Pellow made it a much stronger book. At UC Davis, my undergraduate and graduate students and postdoctoral scholars are also part of this book. They, with my faculty colleagues, have listened, pushed back, and asked questions for the more than ten years of work in the Central Valley that this book covers. Thanks also to Brennan Baraban for his assistance.

I've given talks on this material at a number of institutions and in different contexts. I learned from each at UC Santa Barbara, Claremont McKenna, Cal-State Stanislaus, UC Berkeley, Cornell, Yale, University of Washington, University of Michigan, University of Colorado–Boulder, Arizona State, and the Royal Institute of Technology (Sweden). The Rachel Carson Center for Environment and Society (a joint initiative of Munich's Ludwig-Maximilians-Universität and the Deutsches Museum) was instrumental, through its writing fellowship.

There are so many individuals and organizations to thank: fellow travelers and friends. Activists and scholars in different places and contexts have inspired me to no end. The proceeds from this book will go to the Community Water Center (CWC) in Visalia and UPROSE in New York. Their work on water and climate justice is much needed.

I learned in the late 1990s to be an organizer and an engaged scholar. These are lessons I have taken to heart. I write this book to join you in imagining a more just future.

Lastly, to my husband, Sasha Abramsky, who knows a lot about history and injustice and cares so deeply about the pain of others, meditate more. We need you—not just your writing, but you! To Sofia and Leo, always, for you ... with love.

NOTES

INTRODUCTION

1. American Studies Association call, 2008, https://www.theasa.net/annual-meeting/past-meetings.

2. George Lipsitz, in *Dangerous Crossroads: Popular Music, Postmodernism, and the Poetics of Place* (New York: Verso, 1994), argues that (then) new circuits of economic investment and technological communication erased common-sense notions of place and local identity. Lipsitz asked almost a decade later, "What becomes of 'national knowledge' in our age of globalization?," in *American Studies in a Moment of Danger* (Minneapolis: University of Minnesota Press, 2001).

3. David Harvey, *A Brief History of Neoliberalism* (Oxford: Oxford University Press, 2005), 17.

4. Rupert Neate, "Bill Gates, Jeff Bezos and Warren Buffet Are Wealthier Than Poorest Half of US," *Guardian*, November 8, 2017, https://www.theguardian.com/business/2017/nov/08/bill-gates-jeff-bezos-warren-buffett-wealthier-than-poorest-half-of-us.

5. Graeme Wearden, "Oxfam: 85 Richest People as Wealthy as Poorest Half of the World," *Guardian*, January 20, 2014, https://www.theguardian.com/business/2014/jan/20/oxfam-85-richest-people-half-of-the-world.

6. "Working for the Few," Oxfam, last modified January 20, 2014, https://www.oxfam.org/en/research/working-few.

7. "NOAA: 2017 Was 3rd Warmest Year on Record for the Globe," U.S. Department of Commerce, National Oceanic and Atmospheric Administration, last modified January 18, 2018, www.noaa.gov/news /noaa-2017-was-3rd-warmest-year-on-record-for-globe.

8. "Deadly Environment," Global Witness, last modified April 15, 2014, https://www.globalwitness.org/en/campaigns/environmental-activists/deadly-environment.

9. Walter Benjamin, *Illuminations: Essays and Reflections,* trans. Harry Zohn (New York: Schocken, 1969), 155.

10. For a useful history of the term *intersectionality* since its coinage in 1989 by legal scholar Kimberlé Crenshaw, see Jane Coaston, "The Intersectionality Wars," *Vox,* May 28, 2009, https://www.vox.com/the-highlight/2019/5/20/18542843/intersectionality-conservatism-law-race-gender-discrimination.

11. "Principles of Environmental Justice," retrievable at EJNet.org, accessed June 7, 2019, https://www.ejnet.org/ej/principles.html; "Principles of Working Together," retrievable at EJNet.org, accessed September 10, 2018, https://www.ejnet.org/ej/workingtogether.pdf.

12. Julie Sze, "Naming the Problem(s) and Contextualizing 'Just Environmental' Research," *Items,* September 19, 2017, http://items.ssrc.org /naming-the-problems-contextualizing-just-environmental-research.

13. Jill Harrison, *Pesticide Drift and the Pursuit of Environmental Justice* (Cambridge, MA: MIT Press, 2011).

14. D. Schlosberg and L. Collins, "From Environmental to Climate Justice: Climate Change and the Discourse of Environmental Justice," *Wiley Interdisciplinary Reviews: Climate Change 5,* no. 3 (2014): 359–74.

15. Benjamin Pauli, *Flint Fights Back: Environmental Justice and Democracy in the Flint Water Crisis* (Cambridge, MA: MIT Press, 2019).

16. Julie Sze and Jonathan London, "Environmental Justice at the Crossroads," *Sociology Compass* 2, no. 4 (2008): 1331–54, https://doi.org /10.1111/j.1751–9020.2008.00131.x.

17. Quoted by Indigenous scholar Joanne Barker in "The Corporation and the Tribe," *American Indian Quarterly* 39, no. 3 (2015): 243–70.

18. Raj Patel and Jason Moore, *A History of the World in Seven Cheap Things: A Guide to Capitalism, Nature, and the Future of the Planet* (Berkeley: University of California Press, 2018).

19. Malini Ranganathan, "Thinking with Flint: Racial Liberalism and the Roots of an American Water Tragedy," *Capitalism Nature Socialism* 27, no. 3 (2016): 17–33, https://doi.org/10.1080/10455752.2016.1206583.

20. Quoted in Laura Pulido, "Flint Michigan, Environmental Racism and Racial Capitalism." *Capitalism Nature Socialism* 27, no. 3 (2016): 1–16.

21. Patrick Wolfe, *Settler Colonialism and the Transformation of Anthropology: The Politics and Poetics of an Ethnographic Event,* Writing Past Colonialism (London: Cassell, 1998).

22. Daniel Aldana Cohen, "The Last Stimulus," *Jacobin,* August 15, 2017, https://jacobinmag.com/2017/08/the-last-stimulus. Climate justice activists in this vein include groups like the Leap, Global Grassroots Justice Alliance, the Indigenous Environmental Network, the Labor Network for Sustainability, and the Climate Justice Alliance.

23. Patel and Moore, *A History of the World in Seven Cheap Things.*

24. Kyle Powys Whyte, "Indigenous Climate Change Studies: Indigenizing Futures, Decolonizing the Anthropocene," *English Language Notes* 55, nos. 1–2 (2017): 153–62.

25. Raymond Williams, *Marxism and Literature* (Oxford: Oxford University Press, 1977).

26. Daniel Aldana Cohen writes, for example, of a Queers for the Climate group who, during the 2014 People's Climate March, started the hashtag #itgetswetter. Cohen, "It Gets Wetter," *Dissent,* Summer 2017, https://www.dissentmagazine.org/article/it-gets-wetter-kim-stanley-robinson-new-york-2140.

27. Paul Chatterton, David Featherstone, and Paul Routledge, "Articulating Climate Justice in Copenhagen: Antagonism, the Commons, and Solidarity," *Antipode* 45, no. 3 (2013): 602–20, https://doi.org/10.1111/j.1467–8330.2012.01025.x.

28. "Principles of Environmental Justice," retrievable at EJNet.org; Executive Order 12898, "Federal Actions to Address Environmental Justice in Minority Populations and Low-Income Populations," *Federal Register* 59, no. 32 (1994).

29. Studies have documented the "unequal protection" from environmental pollution by local, state, and national regulatory agencies, highlighting disparities faced by minority communities and they led to new policy formations that varied in their success. David M. Konisky, ed., *Failed Promises: Evaluating the Federal Government's Response to Environmental Justice* (Cambridge, MA: MIT Press, 2015).

30. Ruth Wilson Gilmore, *Golden Gulag: Prisons, Surplus, Crisis, and Opposition in Globalizing California* (Berkeley: University of California Press, 2007), 28.

31. Laura Pulido, "Geographies of Race and Ethnicity II: Environmental Racism, Racial Capitalism and State-Sanctioned Violence," *Progress in Human Geography* 41, no. 4 (2017): 524–33, https://doi.org/10.1177/0309132516646495.

32. See, for example, Robin Kelley's history of neoliberalism, accessed June 7, 2019, www.college.ucla.edu/ge/meetings/161021_HIST_12B.pdf.

33. Ian Tyrell, "What, Exactly, Is 'American Exceptionalism'?," *The Week,* October 21, 2016, http://theweek.com/articles/654508/what-exactly-american-exceptionalism.

34. Justin Gillis and Nadja Popovich, "The U.S. Is the Biggest Carbon Polluter in History. It Just Walked Away from the Paris Climate Deal," *New York Times,* June 1, 2017, https://www.nytimes.com/interactive/2017/06/01/climate/us-biggest-carbon-polluter-in-history-will-it-walk-away-from-the-paris-climate-deal.html.

35. Tess Riley, "Just 100 Companies Responsible for 71% of Global Admissions, Study Says," *Guardian,* July 10, 2017, https://www.theguardian.com/sustainable-business/2017/jul/10/100-fossil-fuel-companies-investors-responsible-71-global-emissions-cdp-study-climate-change.

36. Tejvan Pettinger, "Top CO2 Polluters and Highest per Capita," *Economics Help* blog, October 25, 2017, https://www.economicshelp.org/blog/10296/economics/top-co2-polluters-highest-per-capita.

37. There is a left critique of the capitalism that undergirds the Paris Climate Accords. See David Correia, "Climate Revanchism," *Capitalism Nature Socialism* 27, no. 1 (2016): 1–8, https://doi.org/10.1080/10455752.2016.1140379.

38. The International Geosphere-Biosphere Programme (IGBP) published what it calls the Great Acceleration Indicators, which show an uptick in human activity since 1950. The group's data show that "human activity, predominantly the global economic system, is now the prime driver of change in the Earth System (the sum of our planet's interacting physical, chemical, biological and human processes), according to 24 global indicators." IGBP, "Planetary Dashboard Shows Great Acceleration in Human Activity since 1950," January 15, 2015, www.igbp.net/news /pressreleases/pressreleases/planetarydashboardshowsgreatacceleration inhumanactivitysince1950.5.950c2fa1495db7081eb42.html.

39. Richard Johnson, "Optimism of the Intellect? Hegemony and Hope," *Soundings: A Journal of Politics and Culture* 54 (Summer 2013): 51.

40. Ibid., 63.

41. Robin D. G. Kelley, *Freedom Dreams: The Black Radical Imagination* (Boston: Beacon Press, 2002), x.

42. Walidah Imarisha, Robin D. G. Kelley, and Jonathan Horstmann interviewed by *Red Wedge*, "Black Art Matters: A Roundtable on the Black Radical Imagination," *Red Wedge*, July 26, 2016, www .redwedgemagazine.com/online-issue/black-art-matters-roundtable-black-radical-imaginatio.

43. Malini Ranganathan, "The Environment as Freedom: A Decolonial Reimagining," *Items*, June 13, 2017, https://items.ssrc.org /the-environment-as-freedom-a-decolonial-reimagining. Ranganathan discusses Claudia Jones, who wrote a regular newspaper column from 1950 to 1953 called "Half of the World." For more on Jones, see Denise Lynn, "Claudia Jones' Feminist Vision of Emancipation," *Black Perspectives*, September 8, 2016, https://www.aaihs.org/claudia-jones-feminist-vision-of-emancipation.

44. Ronald Sandler and Phaedra Pezzullo, eds., *Environmental Justice and Environmentalism: The Social Justice Challenge to the Environmental Movement* (Cambridge, MA: MIT Press, 2007).

45. Brentin Mock, "How the Sierra Club Learned to Love Immigration," *Colorlines*, May 8, 2013, September 7, 2018, https://www .colorlines.com/articles/how-sierra-club-learned-love-immigration.

46. My intention here is not to cite the Sierra Club as evidence that police violence and environmental issues are one and the same. Rather, it is to show how organizations can shift their own stances based on both internal and external factors. "Sierra Club Statement on Movement for Black Lives Matter Platform," Sierra Club press release, August 2, 2016, https://content.sierraclub.org/press-releases/2016/08/sierra-club-statement-movement-black-lives-platform.

47. U.S. Department of Health and Human Services, Office of Minority Health, "Asthma and African Americans," accessed May 27, 2019, https://minorityhealth.hhs.gov/omh/browse.aspx?lvl=4&lvlid=15.

48. Lindsey Dillon and Julie Sze, "Equality in the Air We Breathe: Police Violence, Pollution, and the Politics of Sustainability," in *Sustainability: Approaches to Environmental Justice and Social Power,* ed. Julie Sze (New York: New York University Press, 2018), 246–70.

49. Charles Blow, "Inequality in the Air We Breathe?," *New York Times,* January 21, 2015, https://www.nytimes.com/2015/01/22/opinion/charles-blow-inequality-in-the-air-we-breathe.html.

50. *How to Let Go of the World and Love All the Things Climate Can't Change,* directed by Josh Fox (Oley, PA: Bullfrog Films, 2017), 127 min.

51. David Gonzalez, "Yolanda Garcia, 53, Dies; A Bronx Community Force," *New York Times,* February 19, 2005, https://www.nytimes.com/2005/02/19/obituaries/yolanda-garcia-53-dies-a-bronx-community-force.html.

52. Melissa Harris-Perry, "Erica Garner Died of a Heart Attack. But It's Racism That's Killing Black Women," *Elle,* January 2, 2018, https://www.elle.com/culture/a14532058/erica-garner-death-black-women-racism.

53. Vivian Wang, "Erica Garner, Activist and Daughter of Eric Garner, Dies at 27," *New York Times,* December 30, 2017, https://www.nytimes.com/2017/12/30/nyregion/erica-garner-dead.html.

54. Langston Hughes, *A New Song* (New York: International Workers Order Press, 1938), 19.

55. Harrison, *Pesticide Drift and the Pursuit of Environmental Justice*

56. Juan Cole, "Gil Scott-Heron Explains 'The Revolution Will Not Be Televised'," *Informed Comment,* July 6, 2013, https://www.juancole.com/2013/07/explains-revolution-televised.html (emphasis added).

57. Kelley, *Freedom Dreams,* 9 (emphasis added).

58. Naomi Klein, *The Shock Doctrine: The Rise of Disaster Capitalism* (New York: Metropolitan Books, 2008); Naomi Klein, *The Battle for Paradise: Puerto Rico Takes On the Disaster Capitalists* (Chicago: Haymarket Books, 2018); Macarena Gómez-Barris, *The Extractive Zone: Social Ecologies and Decolonial Perspectives* (Durham, NC: Duke University Press, 2017), xiii.

59. These decolonial social ecologies come from the "shifting borderlands, queer and nonreproductive worlds of anarchist affiliation ... including experimental film and vernacular performances." Gómez-Barris, *The Extractive Zone,* 9. On anarchism, see Andrew Cornell, *Unruly Equality: U.S. Anarchism in the Twentieth Century* (Berkeley: University of California Press, 2016).

60. Quoted in Kate Bubacz, "What Happened after Standing Rock," *BuzzFeed News,* February 28, 2018, https://www.buzzfeednews.com/article/katebubacz/what-happened-after-standing-rock.

61. Cohen, "It Gets Wetter."

62. The royalties of this book go to two organizations: Community Water Center, which works on water justice in California, and UPROSE, a New York City–based environmental and climate justice organization.

CHAPTER ONE. THIS MOVEMENT OF MOVEMENTS

1. Robert Warrior, "Home/Not Home: Centering American Studies Where We Are," *American Quarterly* 69, no. 2 (2017): 191–219, https://muse.jhu.edu/article/663318.

2. Ethnic Studies scholar Dylan Rodríguez's response to Warrior's address called it a "time-bending, wonderfully defiant narrative of music, freedom, suffering, loss, movement, and inhabitation against everything horrific that is also, indelibly, the 'American' of American studies?" Dylan Rodríguez, "Protective Measures: Reflections on Robert Warrior's 2016 ASA Presidential Address," *American Quarterly* 69, no. 2 (2017): 221–27, https://muse.jhu.edu/article/663319.

3. There are seven nations of the Oceti Sakowin: the Santee Sioux Tribe, the Yankton Sioux Tribe, the Sicangu Oyate, the Lower Brule

Sioux Tribe, the Crow Creek Sioux Tribe, the Cheyenne River Sioux Tribe, and the Standing Rock Sioux Tribe. "Oceti Sakowin," Akta Lakota Museum and Cultural Center, accessed September 10, 2018, http://aktalakota.stjo.org/site/News2?page=NewsArticle&id=8309.

4. The camps included the Red Warrior Camp and Sacred Stone Camp. Jaskiran Dhillon and Nick Estes, "Introduction: Standing Rock, #NoDAPL, and Mni Wiconi," *Hot Spots* (Society for Cultural Anthropology), December 22, 2016, https://culanth.org/fieldsights/1007-introduction-standing-rock-nodapl-and-mni-wiconi.

5. Jack Healy, "From 280 Tribes, a Protest on the Plains," *New York Times,* September 11, 2016, https://www.nytimes.com/interactive/2016/09/12/us/12tribes.html.

6. For example, one person arrested was Ta'Sina Sapa win. Win been an activist since she was fifteen years old. She was on the front lines of the #NoDAPL movement at Standing Rock, where she was one of the Water Protectors bitten by a private security force dog. See Bubacz, "What Happened after Standing Rock."

7. White House, Office of the Press Secretary, "Construction of the Dakota Access Pipeline," last modified January 24, 2017. https://earthjustice.org/sites/default/files/files/Construction-of-the-Dakota-Access-Pipeline.pdf.

8. Natasha Lennard, "Still Fighting at Standing Rock," *Esquire,* September 19, 2017, https://www.esquire.com/news-politics/a12181154/still-fighting-at-standing-rock.

9. Elizabeth Hoover. *The River Is in Us: Fighting Toxics in a Mohawk Community* (Minnesota: University of Minnesota Press, 2017), 9.

10. Julian Brave NoiseCat and Anne Spice, "A History and Future of Resistance," *Jacobin,* September 8, 2016, https://www.jacobinmag.com/2016/09/standing-rock-dakota-access-pipeline-protest.

11. Valerie Volcovici, "Trump Advisors Aim to Privatize Oil-Rich Indian Reservations," Reuters, December 5, 2016, https://www.reuters.com/article/us-usa-trump-tribes-insight/trump-advisors-aim-to-privatize-oil-rich-indian-reservations-idUSKBN13U1B1.

12. Irene Banos Ruiz, "Granting Indigenous Land Rights Could Save the Climate—or Not," Deutsche Welle, December 5, 2017. www.dw

.com/en/granting-indigenous-land-rights-could-save-the-climate-or-not
/a-38819147.

13. In the United States, the land that the government pushed Native nations onto was historically seen as empty and worthless, what Traci Voyles and Valerie Kuletz call wastelands, only later to have valuable natural resources discovered there. Traci Brynne Voyles, *Wastelanding* (Minneapolis: University of Minnesota Press, 2015); Valerie Kuletz, *The Tainted Desert: Environmental and Social Ruin in the American West* (London: Routledge, 1998).

14. Candis Callison, *How Climate Change Comes to Matter: The Communal Life of Facts* (Durham, NC: Duke University Press, 2014).

15. Johnson, "Optimism of the Intellect?" 57.

16. Dylan A. T. Miner, *Indigenous Aesthetics: Art, Activism and Autonomy* (New York: Bloomsbury, 2017).

17. Their account is based on iconic case studies they were involved in as activist lawyers (Cole in Kettleman City, California; Foster in Chester, Pennsylvania). Luke W. Cole and Sheila R. Foster, *From the Ground Up: Environmental Racism and the Rise of the Environmental Justice Movement* (New York: New York University Press, 2001).

18. Sociologist David Pellow, in *Critical Environmental Justice Studies* (Cambridge: Polity, 2017), argues that the policy focus of environmental justice organizations and reliance on the state have limits. Laura Pulido Pulido, Ellen Kohl, and Nicole-Marie Cotton argue similarly in "State Regulation and Environmental Justice: The Need for Strategy Reassessment," *Capitalism Nature Socialism* 27, no. 2 (2017): 12–31, https://doi.org/10.1080/10455752.2016.1146782.

19. NoiseCat and Spice, "A History and Future of Resistance."

20. Glen Coulthard, "For Our Nations to Live, Capitalism Must Die," Unsettling America, November 5, 2013, https://unsettlingamerica.wordpress.com/2013/11/05/for-our-nations-to-live-capitalism-must-die.

21. Pellow, *Critical Environmental Justice Studies.*

22. "Principles of Environmental Justice," retrievable at EJNet.org.

23. Dana Alston quoted in Robert Gottlieb, *Forcing the Spring: The Transformation of the American Environmental Movement,* rev. and updated ed. (Washington, DC: Island Press, 2005), 34.

24. "Jemez Principles for Democratic Organizing," Southwest Network for Environmental and Economic Justice (SNEEJ), Jemez, New Mexico, December 1996, retreivable at EJNet.org, https://www .ejnet.org/ej/jemez.pdf; "Principles of Working Together," retreivable at EJNet.org; "Principles of the Youth Environmental Justice Movement," the Second National People of Color Environmental Leadership Summit, Washington, D.C., October 26, 2002, retrievable at EJNet.org, https://www.ejnet.org/ej/youthprinciples.pdf; "Bali Principles of Climate Justice," August 29, 2002, retreivable at EJNet.org, https://www.ejnet.org/ej/bali.pdf; "Principles of Climate Justice," Environmental Justice Leadership Forum on Climate Change, 2008, retrievable at EJNet.org, https://www.ejnet.org/ej/ejlf.pdf.

25. IEN was founded as an international coalition based in Bemidji, Minnesota, and began as a struggle to fight a toxic waste incinerator in a Navajo town in Arizona. Cole and Foster, *From the Ground Up,* 134. Shelley Streeby documents the trajectory of IEN, including conferences and gatherings like the 1990 meeting of Indigenous peoples throughout the Western Hemisphere that led to the Declaration of Quito. The declaration reads: "We Indian Peoples consider it vital to defend and conserve our natural resources which are now being attacked by transnational corporations." Shelley Streeby, *Imagining the Future of Climate Change: World-Making through Science Fiction and Activism* (Berkeley: University of California Press, 2018), 60.

26. Indigenous Environmental Network (IEN), accessed September 10, 2018, www.ienearth.org.

27. There is a vast literature on this topic, but one good scholar to start with is Indigenous philosopher Kyle Whyte. See, for example, his article "The Dakota Access Pipeline, Environmental Injustice, and U.S. Colonialism," *Red Ink: An International Journal of Indigenous Literature, Arts, and Humanities* 19, no. 1 (2017): 154–69.

28. Carla Javier, "A Timeline of the Year of Resistance at Standing Rock," *Splinter,* December 14, 2016, https://splinternews.com/a-timeline-of-the-year-of-resistance-at-standing-rock-1794269727.

29. Hydraulic fracturing, commonly called fracking, is a drilling technique used for extracting oil or natural gas from deep underground. Critics say that fracking can destroy drinking water supplies,

pollute the air, contribute to the greenhouse gases that cause global warming, and trigger earthquakes. Marc Lallanilla, "Facts about Fracking," *Live Science,* February 9, 2018, https://www.livescience.com/34464-what-is-fracking.html; "Coalition Members," Americans Against Fracking, accessed September 10, 2018, https://www.americansagainstfracking.org/about-the-coalition/members.

30. NYC Stands with Standing Rock Collective, "#StandingRock-Syllabus," last modified September 5, 2016, https://nycstandswith standingrock.wordpress.com/standingrocksyllabus.

31. "Native Youth Run 2,000 Miles to Washington DC to Protest Dakota Access Pipeline," *Indian Country Today,* August 5, 2016, https://indiancountrymedianetwork.com/news/environment/native-youth-run-2000-miles-to-washington-dc-to-protest-dakota-access-pipeline.

32. In the first six months of DAPL, there were five minor spills, and a federal judge sided with the tribe in pressing for additional anti-spill measures in light of a major Keystone XL spill. "Citing Recent Keystone Spill, Federal Court Orders Additional Measures to Reduce Spill Risks from Dakota Access Pipeline," Earthjustice, December 4, 2017, https://earthjustice.org/news/press/2017/citing-recent-keystone-spill-federal-court-orders-additional-measures-to-reduce-spill-risks-from-dakota-access; Standing Rock Sioux Tribe, "Impacts of an Oil Spill from the Dakota Access Pipeline on the Standing Rock Sioux Tribe," February 21, 2018, https://www.standingrock.org/sites/default/files/uploads/srst_impacts_of_an_oil_spill_2.21.2018.pdf; Wes Enzinna, "'I Didn't Come Here to Lose': How a Movement Was Born at Standing Rock," *Mother Jones,* January/February 2017, https://www.motherjones.com/politics/2016/12/dakota-access-pipeline-standing-rock-oil-water-protest.

33. Robinson Meyer, "Trump's Dakota Access Pipeline Memo: What We Know Right Now," *Atlantic,* January 24, 2017, https://www.theatlantic.com/science/archive/2017/01/trumps-dakota-access-pipeline-memo-what-we-know-right-now/514271.

34. "Updates and Frequently Asked Questions: The Standing Rock Sioux Tribe's Litigation on the Dakota Access Pipeline," Earthjustice, accessed December 4, 2017, https://earthjustice.org/features/faq-standing-rock-litigation#documents.

35. The "#StandingRockSyllabus," compiled by the NYC Stands with Standing Rock Collective contributors, is massive. The longer version is more than 2,400 pages. See also Nick Estes and Jaskiran Dhillon, eds., *Standing with Standing Rock: Voices from the #NoDAPL Movement* (Minneapolis: University of Minnesota Press, 2019).

36. NoiseCat and Spice, "A History and Future of Resistance"; Eve Tuck and K. Wayne Yang, "Decolonization Is Not a Metaphor," *Decolonization: Indigeneity, Education and Society* 1, no. 1 (2012): 1–40.

37. Dhillon and Estes, "Introduction: Standing Rock, #NoDAPL, and Mni Wiconi."

38. Ibid.

39. The Dawes Allotment Act of 1887 (which allowed individual tribesmen to own land) and the creation of five smaller reservations further factionalized the Oceti Sakowin. See Dhillon and Estes, "Introduction: Standing Rock, #NoDAPL, and Mni Wiconi."

40. Followers of the Ghost Dance danced in circles until they collapsed into trances. The U.S. Army killed more than 200 Lakota Sioux at Wounded Knee Creek in 1890 (officially, 146 went into the mass grave, but many others died later from wounds and/or exposure). The Ghost Dance has been viewed as an effort by Indian militants to resist American conquest and return to traditional ways. Recent scholarship suggests that the followers of the Ghost Dance were also engaged deeply with modernity. See also Louis Warren, *God's Red Son: The Ghost Dance Religion and the Making of Modern America* (New York: Basic Books, 2017).

41. Maria Streshinsky, "Saying No to $1 Billion," *Atlantic,* March 2011, https://www.theatlantic.com/magazine/archive/2011/03/saying-no-to-1-billion/308380.

42. The Oceti Sakowin unified despite attempts to divide and conquer. Groups such as the National Indian Youth Council and the American Indian Movement formed in the urban centers to combat the wholesale destruction of Native life on- and off-reservation. See Estes and Dhillon, eds., *Standing with Standing Rock;* and Nick Estes, *Our History Is the Future: Standing Rock versus the Dakota Access Pipeline, and the Long Tradition of Indigenous Resistance* (New York: Random House, 2019).

43. Nick Estes, "Fighting for Our Lives: #NoDAPL in Historical Context," *Red Nation,* September 18, 2016, https://therednation.org/2016/09/18/fighting-for-our-lives-nodapl-in-context.

44. "In Conversation: Standing with Standing Rock," Earthjustice, accessed September 10, 2018, https://earthjustice.org/features/teleconference-standing-rock#events.

45. Catherine Thorbecke, "Why a Previously Proposed Route for the Dakota Access Pipeline Was Rejected," *ABC News,* November 3, 2016, https://abcnews.go.com/US/previously-proposed-route-dakota-access-pipeline-rejected/story?id=43274356.

46. *Founding Sacred Stone Camp,* We Are the Media, Facebook video, 2016, 1 min., 37 sec., https://www.facebook.com/wearethemedia2016/videos/652593478255016; Streeby, *Imagining the Future of Climate Change,* 37.

47. Sacred Stone Camp zine, n.d., https://d3n8a8pro7vhmx.cloudfront.net/honorearth/pages/2267/attachments/original/1470612897/ND_ZINE_updated.pdf?1470612897.

48. Hoover, *The River Is in Us,* 12.

49. Saul Elbein, "These Are the Defiant 'Water Protectors' of Standing Rock," *National Geographic,* January 26, 2017, https://news.nationalgeographic.com/2017/01/tribes-standing-rock-dakota-access-pipeline-advancement.

50. *Founding Sacred Stone Camp,* We Are the Media, Facebook video.

51. LaDonna Brave Bull Allard, "Why the Founder of Standing Rock Sioux Camp Can't Forget the Whitestone Massacre," *Yes!,* September 3, 2016, www.yesmagazine.org/people-power/why-the-founder-of-standing-rock-sioux-camp-cant-forget-the-whitestone-massacre-20160903.

52. Quoted in Saul Elbein, "The Youth Group That Launched a Movement at Standing Rock," *New York Times,* January 31, 2017, https://www.nytimes.com/2017/01/31/magazine/the-youth-group-that-launched-a-movement-at-standing-rock.html.

53. "Native Youth Run 2,000 Miles to Washington DC to Protest Dakota Access Pipeline."

54. Indigenous youth are well-represented in the landmark children's lawsuit on climate change. Our Children's Trust, accessed September 10, 2018, https://www.ourchildrenstrust.org.

55. Jaskiran Dhillon, "Indigenous Youth Are Building a Climate Justice Movement by Targeting Colonialism," *Truthout,* June 20, 2016, https://truthout.org/articles/indigenous-youth-are-building-a-climate-justice-movement-by-targeting-colonialism.

56. Alexis Celeste Bunten, "Indigenous Resistance: The Big Picture behind Pipeline Protests," *Cultural Survival,* March 2017, https://www.culturalsurvival.org/publications/cultural-survival-quarterly/indigenous-resistance-big-picture-behind-pipeline-protests. In "The Corporation and the Tribe," Joanne Barker (Lenape) explains the historical links between the U.S. government and corporations, looking at the foundational legal definitions of the corporation and the tribe between 1790 and 1887.

57. Quoted in Dhillon and Estes, "Introduction: Standing Rock, #NoDAPL, and Mni Wiconi" (emphasis in original).

58. Allard, 2016.

59. Layli Long Soldier, Camille Seaman, Deborah A. Miranda, Toni Jensen, Jennifer Elise Foerster, Heid Erdrich, Natalie Diaz, Louise Erdrich, and Joy Harjo, "Women and Standing Rock," *Orion,* accessed September 10, 2018, https://orionmagazine.org/article/women-standing-rock.

60. Quoted in Karen Pauls, "'We must kill the black snake': Prophecy and Prayer Motivate Standing Rock Movement," *CBC News,* December 11, 2016, www.cbc.ca/news/canada/manitoba/dakota-access-pipeline-prayer-1.3887441.

61. Traci Brynne Voyles, "Man Destroys Nature? Gender, History, and the Feminist Praxis of Situating Sustainability," in *Sustainability: Approaches to Environmental Justice and Social Power,* edited by Julie Sze (New York: NYU Press, 2018), 196–221.

62. Quoted in Jack Healy, "From 280 Tribes, a Protest on the Plains," *New York Times,* September 11, 2016, https://www.nytimes.com/interactive/2016/09/12/us/12tribes.html.

63. Quoted in Natalie Zisa, "Meet the 23-Year-Old Who's Helping Lead the Indigenous Resistance against Pipelines," Brit+Co, January 8, 2018, https://www.brit.co/jackie-fielder-indigenous-resistance-against-pipelines. Some women central to #NoDAPL include Tara Houska (Ani-

shinaabe/Couchiching First Nation), a tribal rights attorney; Michelle Cook (Navajo), a human rights lawyer, and LaDonna Brave Bull Allard.

64. Bubacz, "What Happened after Standing Rock."

65. This relationship is described in the 2016 report *Violence on the Land, Violence on Our Bodies: Building an Indigenous Response to Environmental Violence,* written by the Native Youth Sexual Health Network (NYSHN) in partnership with Women's Earth Alliance, http://landbodydefense .org. NYSHN is a grassroots network by and for Indigenous youth that works across issues of sexual and reproductive health, rights, and justice in the United States and Canada.

66. Dhillon, "Indigenous Youth Are Building a Climate Justice Movement by Targeting Colonialism."

67. Julia Carrie Wong, "Dakota Access Pipeline: 300 Protesters Injured after Police Use Water Cannons," *Guardian,* November 21, 2016, https://www.theguardian.com/us-news/2016/nov/21/dakota-access-pipeline-water-cannon-police-standing-rock-protest.

68. Joshua Barajas, "Police Deploy Water Hoses, Tear Gas against Standing Rock Protesters," *PBS NewsHour,* November 21, 2016, https://www.pbs.org/newshour/nation/police-deploy-water-hoses-tear-gas-against-standing-rock-protesters; Julia Carrie Wong and Sam Levin, "Standing Rock Protesters Hold Out against Extraordinary Police Violence," *Guardian,* November 29, 2016, https://www.theguardian .com/us-news/2016/nov/29/standing-rock-protest-north-dakota-shutdown-evacuation.

69. Sam Levin, "Dakota Pipeline Protesters Say Activist Accused of Shooting at Police Is a Pacifist," *Guardian,* November 3, 2016, https://www.theguardian.com/us-news/2016/nov/03/dakota-pipeline-activist-red-fawn-fallis-accused-shooting-police-pacifist; Sandy Tolan, "Journalist Faces Charges after Arrest while Covering Dakota Access Pipeline Protest," *LA Times,* February 5, 2017, http://www.latimes.com/nation /la-na-standing-rock-journalist-arrest-20170205-story.html.

70. Mark Hand, "Native Americans Who Protested Dakota Access Get Handed the Longest Prison Sentences," *Think Progress,* July 12, 2018, https://thinkprogress.org/native-americans-who-protested-dakota-access-get-handed-the-longest-prison-sentences-e7510ca5f2d7.

71. Natasha Lennard, "Still Fighting at Standing Rock," *Esquire*, September 19, 2017, https://www.esquire.com/news-politics/a12181154 /still-fighting-at-standing-rock.

72. Christopher Ingraham, "Republican Lawmakers Introduce Bills to Curb Protesting in at Least 18 States," *Washington Post*, February 24, 2017, https://www.washingtonpost.com/news/wonk/wp/2017 /02/24/republican-lawmakers-introduce-bills-to-curb-protesting-in-at-least-17-states/?utm_term=.dc45da30cdd4.

73. Brian Hauss, "Standing Rock Protest Groups Sued by Dakota Access Pipeline Company," ACLU blog, December 6, 2017, https:// www.aclu.org/blog/free-speech/rights-protesters/standing-rock-protest-groups-sued-dakota-access-pipeline-company.

74. In Canada, local, regional and national police, and military and intelligence agencies worked together against Indigenous protest movements like Idle No More. Jorge Barrera, "Federal Officials Discussed Raising Alert Level to Highest Level during Idle No More, Book Says," *CBC News*, March 1, 2018, www.cbc.ca/news/indigenous/security-indigenous-alert-level-1.4556618.

75. Ashoka Jegroo, "Why Black Lives Matter Is Fighting Alongside Dakota Access Pipeline Protests," *Splinter*, September 13, 2016, https:// splinternews.com/why-black-lives-matter-is-fighting-alongside-dakota-acc-1793861838.

76. Leanne Simpson, "An Indigenous View on #BlackLivesMatter," *Yes!*, December 5, 2014, http://www.yesmagazine.org/peace-justice/indigenous-view-black-lives-matter-leanne-simpson.

77. Quoted in Kara Weisenstein, "How Art Immortalized #NoDAPL Protests at Standing Rock," *Vice*, February 28, 2017, https:// www.vice.com/en_us/article/d334ba/how-art-immortalized-nodapl-protests-at-standing-rock (emphasis added).

78. Imarisha, Kelley, and Horstmann interviewed by *Red Wedge*, "Black Art Matters: A Roundtable on the Black Radical Imagination" (emphasis added).

79. Elbein, "These Are the Defiant 'Water Protectors' of Standing Rock."

80. *Mother Jones* has reported on various tensions between Native and white activists over tactics, appropriation, and other issues. Enzinna, "'I Didn't Come Here to Lose': How a Movement Was Born at Standing Rock."

81. Bubacz, "What Happened after Standing Rock."

82. Palestinians Stand with Standing Rock," Palestinian Youth Movement, accessed September 10, 2018, www.pymusa.com/from-standing-rock-to-palestine; Rick Kearns, "Solidarity from the South: Indigenous Leaders from Ecuador Come to Standing Rock," *Indian Country Today,* October 1, 2016, https://indiancountrymedianetwork.com/news/indigenous-peoples/solidarity-from-the-south-indigenous-leaders-from-ecuador-come-to-standing-rock; Sam Levin, "Army Veterans Return to Standing Rock to Form a Human Shield against Police," *Guardian,* February 11, 2017, https://www.theguardian.com/us-news/2017/feb/11/standing-rock-army-veterans-camp; Adam Linehan, "Why They Went: The Inside Story of the Standing Rock Veterans," *Task and Purpose,* December 19, 2016, https://taskandpurpose.com/went-inside-story-standing-rock-veterans.

83. Grassrope dismisses as "colonized thinking" the arguments of those who believe the tribes can win with violence. Quoted in Elbein, "These Are the Defiant 'Water Protectors' of Standing Rock."

84. Kate Schimel, "How the Keep It in the Ground Movement Came to Be," *High Country News,* July 19, 2016, https://www.hcn.org/articles/how-the-keep-it-in-the-ground-movement-gained-momentum.

85. "Keep It in the Ground," Indigenous Environmental Network, accessed September 10, 2018, www.ienearth.org/?s=Keep+It+in+the+Ground.

86. Peter Newell and Dustin Mulvaney, "The Political Economy of the 'Just Transition,'" *Geographical Journal* 179, no. 2 (2013): 132–40, https://rgs-ibg.onlinelibrary.wiley.com/doi/abs/10.1111/geoj.12008.

87. Caroline Farrell, "A Just Transition: Lessons Learned from the Environmental Justice Movement," *Duke Forum for Law and Social Change* 4 (2012): 45–63.

88. Julie Sze and Elizabeth Yeampierre, "Towards a Just Transition: Climate Justice, Development and Community Resilience," in

Just Green Enough: Urban Development and Environmental Gentrification, ed. Winifred Curren and Trina Hamilton (New York: Routledge, 2018), 61–67.

89. "Indigenous Principles of Just Transition," Indigenous Environmental Network, accessed May 12, 2019, www.ienearth.org/justtransition. Additional principles, especially important in light of Standing Rock and other pipeline battles, read:

> A Just Transition acknowledges the Earth is a living female organism— our Mother. Water is her lifeblood. The Earth and Father Sky, with its air and atmosphere, are the source of life to be protected, not merely a resource to be exploited, degraded, privatized and commodified.
>
> A Just Transition recognizes that strategies were first forged by labor unions and environmental justice groups, rooted in people of color and low-income communities as well as Indigenous lands; who jointly saw the need to phase out industries that were polluting workers, community and Mother Earth; and at the same time provide just pathways for workers to transition to other jobs. It was rooted in workers defining a transition away from toxic polluting industries in alliances with fence line and frontline communities.

90. Long Soldier et al., "Women and Standing Rock."

91. Sarain Fox describes the Art Action camp in Weisenstein, "How Art Immortalized #NoDAPL Protests at Standing Rock":

> The Art Action Camp was made up of four components: the artists who are creating, the legal team who is there to consult and inform people of risks before they go out, the media team—which I was a part of—who helps navigate press releases and how to communicate with the media, and then the action team who actually plans and strategizes.

92. See Justseeds Artists' Cooperative statement, accessed April 19, 2019, https://justseeds.org/about.

93. Quoted in Bubacz, "What Happened after Standing Rock."

94. Neil deMause, "As Industry City Promises a New Sunset Park, Some Residents Fight to Maintain the Old One," *City Limits,* October 27, 2015, https://citylimits.org/2015/10/27/as-industry-city-promises-a-new-sunset-park-some-residents-fight-to-maintain-the-old-one.

95. "Climate Justice Center," UPROSE, accessed September 10, 2018, https://www.uprose.org/climate-justice.

96. Sze and Yeampierre, "Towards a Just Transition."

97. "Youth Organizing," UPROSE, accessed September 10, 2018, https://www.uprose.org/youth-summit-2017.

98. Ellie Shechet, "At a Climate Justice Fashion Show, the Kids Prove They're Gonna Be All Right, Jezebel," last modified August 4, 2017,https://themuse.jezebel.com/at-a-climate-justice-fashion-show-the-kids-prove-theyr-1797517543.

99. Wilbur and the subsequent statements from Pike, Allard, and Goldtooth are quoted in Bubacz, "What Happened after Standing Rock" (emphasis added).

100. Jegroo, 2016.

CHAPTER TWO. ENVIRONMENTAL JUSTICE ENCOUNTERS

Epigraph: Martin Luther King Jr., "The Quest for Peace and Justice," December 11, 1964, Nobel lecture, https://www.nobelprize.org/prizes /peace/1964/king/lecture.

1. Children with low levels of lead exposure have higher rates of behavioral problems (hyperactivity and trouble concentrating), problems with impulse control, lower scores on standardized tests, higher rates of juvenile delinquency and higher rates of adult arrests and unemployment and of kidney and heart disorders. Gerald Markowitz and David Rosner, *Lead Wars: The Politics of Science and the Fate of America's Children* (Berkeley: University of California Press, 2013), 15–16.

2. In "Water Marginalization at the Urban Fringe: Environmental Justice and Urban Political Ecology across the North–South Divide," *Urban Geography* 36, no. 3 (2015): 403–23, authors Malini Ranganathan and Carolina Balazs talk of "staging an encounter" between vastly different sites.

3. Carolina Balazs, Rachel Morello-Frosch, Alan Hubbard, and Isha Ray, "Social Disparities in Nitrate Contaminated Drinking Water in the San Joaquin Valley," *Environmental Health Perspectives* 119, no. 9 (2011): 1272–78; Carolina Balazs and Isha Ray, "The Drinking

Water Disparities Framework: On the Origins and Persistence of Inequities in Exposure," *American Journal of Public Health*104, no. 4 (2014): 603–11.

4. *The Human Costs of Nitrate-Contaminated Drinking Water in the San Joaquin Valley* (Oakland: Pacific Institute, 2011), retrievable at http://d3n8a8pro7vhmx.cloudfront.net/communitywatercenter/pages/36/attachments/original/1394234487/PacInst_Human-Costs-of-Nitrate_2011.pdf?1394234487.

5. Patricia Leigh Brown, "The Flint of California," *Politico,* May 25, 2016,https://www.politico.com/agenda/story/2016/05/is-clean-drinking-water-a-right-000129.

6. Andrew R. Highsmith, *Demolition Means Progress: Flint, Michigan, and the Fate of the American Metropolis* (Chicago: University of Chicago Press, 2015), 1.

7. John Eligon, "A Question of Environmental Racism in Flint," *New York Times,* January 21, 2016, https://www.nytimes.com/2016/01/22/us/a-question-of-environmental-racism-in-flint.html.

8. Pauli, *Flint Fights Back,* 102.

9. Stuart Hall, Doreen Massey, and Michael Rustin, eds., *After Neoliberalism? The Kilburn Manifesto* (London: Lawrence and Wishart, 2015), 14–15.

10. Lawyer and journalist Carey McWilliams's 1939 classic study, *Factories in the Field,* described a landscape that differs from today's agricultural industry only in the demographics of the migratory farm labor population.

11. Jill Harrison studies contemporary pesticide drift activism, policy, and science. Pesticide poisoning is both pervasive and invisible, similar to how lead poisoning persists in the United States. See her *Pesticide Drift and the Pursuit of Environmental Justice* (Cambridge, MA: MIT Press, 2011).

12. Chelsea Grimmer, "Racial Microbiopolitics: Flint Lead Poisoning, Detroit Water Shut Offs, and the 'Matter' of Enfleshment," *Comparitist* 41 (2017): 23–24, https://muse.jhu.edu/article/675731.

13. Rob Nixon, *Slow Violence and the Environmentalism of the Poor* (Cambridge, MA: Harvard University Press, 2011), 2.

14. In *Slow Violence and the Environmentalism of the Poor,* Nixon writes that "violence is customarily conceived as an event that is immediate in time, explosive and spectacular in space, and as erupting into instant sensational visibility" (2).

15. Chloe Ahmann, "'It's exhausting to create an event out of nothing': Slow Violence and the Manipulation of Time," *Cultural Anthropology* 33, no. 1 (2018): 142–71, quote on 164–65. Ahmann further writes that "slow violence is a condition that seems to invite incoherence. It takes too long, it's hard to notice, and it casts a wide chasm between effects and the various forces to which we might attribute cause. But it is, in fact, an object" (164).

16. The Little River Band of Ottawa donated $10,000 to Flint, based on their conception of water as a gift. "Little River Band of Ottawa Give $10K to Assist in Flint Water Crisis," *Native News Online,* January 19, 2016, http://nativenewsonline.net/currents/23974.

17. In 2014, forty-six thousand shutoff notices were sent to Detroit households for nonpayment of bills. For residents and activists, it is a serious issue when the city's poorest, including children, are made to live without running water in their homes. A group of United Nations experts called it a violation of human rights. Kate Abbey-Lambertz, "How Detroit's Water Crisis Is Part of a Much Bigger Problem," *Huffington Post,* August 19, 2014, https://www.huffingtonpost.com/2014/08/19/detroit-water-shutoffs_n_5690980.html.

18. The California declaration is largely symbolic, intended as a moral compass for water policy. It does contain a key provision requiring state agencies to consider the human right to water when establishing new regulations and grant programs. Brown, "The Flint of California."

19. Mona Hanna-Attisha, *What the Eyes Don't See: A Story of Crisis, Resistance, and Hope in an American City* (New York: Random House, 2018).

20. William Finnegan, "Flint and the Long Struggle against Lead Poisoning," *New Yorker,* February 4, 2016, https://www.newyorker.com/news/daily-comment/flint-and-the-long-struggle-against-lead-poisoning. Experts who raised alarms included Miguel Del Toral from the Environmental Protection Agency; Hanna-Attisha, a young Flint pediatrician, who documented the rise in childhood lead

poisoning; and Marc Edwards, a civil-engineering professor at Virginia Tech.

21. KWA was incorporated in 2010 and began its first fiscal year on October 1, 2010. See Peter J. Hammer, "The Flint Water Crisis, the Karegnondi Water Authority and Strategic-Structural Racism," *Critical Sociology* 45, no. 1 (2019): 103–19.

22. Amy Davidson Sorkin, "The Contempt That Poisoned Flint's Water," *New Yorker,* January 22, 2016, https://www.newyorker.com /news/amy-davidson/the-contempt-that-poisoned-flints-water.

23. Quoted in Graham Cassano and Teressa A. Benz, "Introduction: Flint and the Racialized Geography of Indifference," *Critical Sociology* 45, no. 1 (2019): 25–32.

24. Kyle T. Mays, "Flint: Not Just a Black Issue," *Indian Country Today,* January 25, 2016, https://indiancountrymedianetwork.com/news /opinions/flint-not-just-a-black-issue.

25. The 1819 Treaty of Saginaw ceded more than six million acres of land when the first white settler in Flint, Jacob Smith, signed away the land in return for a cash payment and land for his children. His descendants used the court system to further deterritorialize the Anishinaabeg, who lost more than seven thousand acres along the Flint River. Dylan Miner, *Tikibiing Booskikamigaag: An Indigenous History and Ecology of Flint,* 24-page limited edition artist's book (N.p.: Dylan Miner, 2013).

26. Christopher F. Petrella and Ameer Loggins, "Standing Rock, Flint, and the Color of Water," *Black Perspectives,* November 2, 2016, https://www.aaihs.org/standing-rock-flint-and-the-color-of-water.

27. Kyle T. Mays, "From Flint to Standing Rock: The Aligned Struggles of Black and Indigenous People," *Cultural Anthropology,* December 22, 2016, https://culanth.org/fieldsights/from-flint-to-standing-rock-the-aligned-struggles-of-black-and-indigenous-people.

28. Jamie Peck, "Austerity Urbanism," *City* 16, no. 6 (2012): 626–55, https://doi.org/10.1080/13604813.2012.734071 (emphasis added).

29. "GM tried not only to defeat workers but also the environment in which they, and all of us, live … linked by roads, rivers and streams.… Flint and the area around it had become an industrially polluted landscape (dependent on lead)." Gerald Rosner, "Flint, Mich-

igan: A Century of Environmental Injustice," *American Journal of Public Health* 106, no. 2 (February 2016): 200–201.

30. Emily L. Dawson, "Lessons Learned from Flint, Michigan: Managing Multiple Source Pollution in Urban Communities," *William and Mary Environmental Law and Policy Review* 26, no. 2 (2001): 367–405, http://scholarship.law.wm.edu/wmelpr/vol26/iss2/5; Brandon Ward, "The Promise of Jobs: Blackmail and Environmental Justice in Flint, Michigan, 1991–1995," *Environmental Justice* 6, no. 5 (2013): 163–68, https:// doi.org/10.1089/env.2013.0030.

31. The percentage of the population of Flint relative to the population of its county, Genesee, has fallen dramatically from just more than half to less than a quarter in the past fifty years. The population of Genesee County is not just whiter than the city of Flint; it is also wealthier. See Hammer, "The Flint Water Crisis."

32. In 1990, 30.6 percent of Flint residents lived below the poverty line. Ibid., 5.

33. Andrew R. Highsmith, "Beyond Corporate Abandonment: General Motors and the Politics of Metropolitan Capitalism in Flint, Michigan," *Journal of Urban History* 40, no. 1 (2014): 31–47, https://doi .org/10.1177/0096144213508080.

34. Highsmith, *Demolition Means Progress*, 130.

35. John Wisely, "Flint Residents Paid America's Highest Water Rates," *Detroit Free Press,* February 16, 2016, https://www.freep.com /story/news/local/michigan/flint-water-crisis/2016/02/16/study-flint-paid-highest-rate-us-water/80461288.

36. Katrease Stafford, "Controversial Water Shutoffs Could Hit 17,461 Detroit Households," *Detroit Free Press,* March 26, 2018, https:// www.freep.com/story/news/local/michigan/detroit/2018/03/26/more-than-17–000-detroit-households-risk-water-shutoffs/452801002; Jacey Fortin, "In Flint, Overdue Bills for Unsafe Water Could Lead to Fore-closures," *New York Times,* May 4, 2017, https://www.nytimes.com /2017/05/04/us/flint-water-home-foreclosure.html.

37. Michigan's Public Act 4 (PA 4) of 2011 significantly expanded the powers of the emergency manager, granting control over all aspects of a city's operations. Carolyn G. Loh, "The Everyday Emergency: Planning

and Democracy under Austerity Regimes," *Urban Affairs Review* 52, no. 5 (2015): 832–63, https://doi.org/10.1177/1078087415577639.

38. The emergency manager assumes authority over all of a jurisdiction's elected and appointed officials, such as hiring and firing, spending money, and making strategic decisions. Additionally, the EM may break union contracts or enter into new ones, sell public assets, and privatize public functions. The EM may prohibit a city council from holding meetings, and if the council nevertheless continues to meet, its actions carry no authority.

39. Fasenfest writes that "if you live in Michigan there is a 10% chance that you have lived under emergency management since 2009. But if you are a black Michigander, the odds are 50/50." David Fasenfest, "A Neoliberal Response to an Urban Crisis: Emergency Management in Flint, MI," *Critical Sociology* 45, no. 1 (2019): 33–47. See also David Fasenfest, *Unelected, Unaccountable: The Impact of Emergency Managers on Key Michigan Cities* (Detroit: ACLU of Michigan, 2017).

40. "Emergency Manager laws reflect a singular approach; specifically, the application of austerity policies that privilege financial rather than a social solution to a community's ills." Fasenfest, "A Neoliberal Response to an Urban Crisis."

41. Ibid.

42. Loh, "The Everyday Emergency," 836–37.

43. Between 2006 and 2012, state revenue sharing and property tax revenue fell 33 percent and income tax revenue by 39 percent. Hammer, "The Flint Water Crisis."

44. Fasenfest, *Unelected, Unaccountable.* This language is part of the playbook of austerity urbanism; see Peck, "Austerity Urbanism."

45. Loh, "The Everyday Emergency," 839; Hammer, "The Flint Water Crisis."

46. At this point, Emergency Manager Kurtz started to strategically remove options from the table to influence the outcome. See Hammer, "The Flint Water Crisis."

47. The DEQ adopted a flawed and indefensible interpretation of the Lead and Copper Rule (LCR) that committed it to engage in two six-month testing periods *before* taking any action with respect to the Flint River, including the recommendation of adding corrosion

control. Hammer, "The Flint Water Crisis." From the standpoint of protecting public safety, it is a bad decision, but it makes perfect sense if the intention is to run twelve months off a time-limited clock.

48. In "The Flint Water Crisis," Hammer writes of a "united front" of the Michigan Treasury approval of the KWA pipeline and manipulation of state rules governing debt limits to finance the pipeline.

49. Dara Lind, "A Barrier to Clean Water in Flint, Michigan: A Government-Issued ID," *Vox,* January 25, 2016, https://www.vox.com /2016/1/25/10827734/flint-water-immigrants.

50. Although criminal indictments were made (including for involuntary manslaughter), ultimately all were dropped. Mitch Smith, "Flint Water Prosecutors Drop Criminal Charges, With Plans to Keep Investigating," *New York Times,* June 13, 2019, https://www.nytimes .com/2019/06/13/us/flint-water-crisis-charges-dropped.html.

51. Michelle Wilde Anderson, "Mapped Out of Local Democracy," *Stanford Law Review* 62, no. 4 (2010): 931–1003..

52. Camille Pannu, "Drinking Water and Exclusion: A Case Study from California's Central Valley," *California Law Review* 100, no. 1 (2012): 223–68, https://doi.org/10.15779/Z38B133.

53. Community Water Center, accessed September 13, 2018, https:// www.communitywatercenter.org.

54. Christopher Sellers, "Piping as Poison: The Flint Water Crisis and America's Toxic Infrastructure," *The Conversation,* January 25, 2016, http://theconversation.com/piping-as-poison-the-flint-water-crisis-and-americas-toxic-infrastructure-53473. See also Christopher Sellers, "The Flint Water Crisis: A Special Edition Environment and Health Roundtable," *Edge Effects,* February 4, 2016, http://edgeeffects .net/flint-water-crisis.

55. Markowitz and Rosner, *Lead Wars.*

56. Nathan Hare, "Black Ecology," *Black Scholar* 1, no. 6 (1970): 2–8, https://doi.org/10.1080/00064246.1970.11728700.

57. Hammer, "The Flint Water Crisis."

58. Quoted in Merrit Kennedy, "Flint Activist Wins Major Environmental Prize," NPR, April 23, 2018, https://www.npr.org /sections/thetwo-way/2018/04/23/604915435/flint-activist-wins-major-environmental-prize.

59. "Flint Water Crisis Fast Facts," *CNN* online, April 8, 2018, https://www.cnn.com/2016/03/04/us/flint-water-crisis-fast-facts/index.html; Siddhartha Roy, "Commentary: MDEQ Mistakes and Deception Created the Flint Water Crisis," Flint Water Study, September 30, 2015, http://flintwaterstudy.org/2015/09/commentary-mdeq-mistakes-deception-flint-water-crisis.

60. Ben Mathis-Lilley, "Michigan Knew Last Year That Flint's Water Might Be Poisoned but Decided Not to Tell Anyone," *Slate,* January 11, 2016, www.slate.com/blogs/the_slatest/2016/01/11/state_of_michigan_flint_broke_law_and_covered_up_lead_levels_in_water_expert.html.

61. Hanna-Attisha, *What the Eyes Don't See.*

62. Grimmer, "Racial Microbiopolitics," 20.

63. Grimmer writes:

> Cities' and business' justification of shut offs or lack of clean water through a rhetoric of uncontainable contagion and/or unworthy debtors makes some lives culturally 'matter' more than others by cutting off or making poisonous the literal matter necessary for those lives to continue. Such a denial regulates literal matter (shut offs) or codes it as unpredictable (lead poisoning), which merges violence at the biological level with a historically material process of producing and expanding capital in post-industrial, neoliberal landscapes. (Ibid., 23)

64. Pauli, *Flint Fights Back,* 233.

65. Balazs and Ray, "The Drinking Water Disparities Framework," 606.

66. Sharon Howell, Michael D. Doan, and Ami Harbin, "Detroit to Flint and Back Again: Solidarity Forever," *Critical Sociology* 45, no. 1 (2019): 63–83.

67. Quoted in profile of Susana De Anda, Petra Leaders for Justice, accessed September 13, 2018, http://petrafoundation.org/fellows/susana-deanda/index.html.

68. Voices from the Valley, accessed September 13, 2018, www.voicesfromthevalley.org.

69. See *Thirsty for Justice: A People's Blueprint for California Water,* Environmental Coalition for Water Justice, accessed April 19, 2019, at http://www.ejcw.org/our_work/blueprint.html.

70. See, for example, John Sullivan, Sharon Petronella, Edward Brooks, Maria Murillo, Loree Primeau, and Jonathan Ward, "Theatre of the Oppressed and Environmental Justice Communities: A Transformational Therapy for the Body Politic," *Journal of Health Psychology* 13, no. 2 (2008): 166–79, https://doi.org/10.1177/1359105307086710. The authors discuss how the National Institute of Environmental Health Sciences Center at the University of Texas Medical Branch used Theatre of the Oppressed in a Houston project called Communities Organized against Asthma and Lead (COAL).

71. TO is a radical process, public event, and performance that "links environmental justice with 'the Dance of Feeling, Science & Story.'" COAL and El Teatro Lucha por la Salud del Barrio worked on a show, tell, and (above all) listening outreach to Latino neighborhoods on Houston's near north side, where asthma rates are disproportionately high. Ibid.

72. Tracy Perkins, "On Becoming a Public Sociologist: Amplifying Women's Voices in the Quest for Environmental Justice," in *Sociologists in Action: Sociology, Social Change, and Social Justice,* ed. Shelley K. White, Jonathan M. White, and Kathleen Odell Korgan (Los Angeles: Sage, 2015), 90.

73. In *Pesticide Drift and the Pursuit of Environmental Justice,* Jill Harrison describes when more than 170 Spanish-speaking residents vomited, could not breathe, had burning eyes and lungs, and experienced dizziness because of a pesticide drift incident. The emergency response personnel did not speak Spanish and brought the most ill residents to the school, stripped them publicly, and sprayed them with hoses. Later, an investigation revealed that a cloud of metam sodium, a soil fumigant that is a known carcinogen, was to blame.

74. Pauli, *Flint Fights Back,* 238.

75. Howell, Doan, and Harbin, "Detroit to Flint and Back Again."

76. Ibid.

77. Ibid.

78. Ibid.

79. Ibid.

80. Ibid.

81. Failed and contentious collaborations are common in environmental justice disputes, including in Flint. Marc Edwards, the Virginia Tech scientist who confirmed the lead poisoning, is now involved in an ugly defamation lawsuit against some local activists. Nidhi Subbaraman, "A Scientist Is Suing Flint Activists for Defamation. They Say His Ego Is Out of Control." *BuzzFeed News,* July 26, 2018, https://www.buzzfeednews.com/article/nidhisubbaraman/marc-edwards-flint-lawsuit.

82. See Pauli, *Flint Fights Back,* 23, especially chapter 7, "The Water Is (Not) Safe: Expertise, Citizen Science, and the Science Wars."

83. Natalie Haddad, "The Politics of Adversity in Pope.L's Flint Water Project," Hyperallergic, October 28, 2017, https://hyperallergic.com/408167/pope-l-flint-water-project-what-pipeline-michigan-2017.

84. Rosemary Feitelberg, "Tracy Reese Teams with Artist Mel Chin for Art Project Designed to Raise Awareness of Flint's Water Crisis," *Women's Wear Daily,* April 6, 2018, https://wwd.com/fashion-news/fashion-scoops/tracy-reese-artist-mel-chin-designed-to-raise-awareness-of-flints-water-crisis-1202645026.

85. "New Documentary on Flint Looks for "Inspiration in the Wake of Desperation,'" Michigan Radio, December 12, 2017, http://michiganradio.org/post/new-documentary-flint-looks-inspiration-wake-desperation.

86. Natasha Thomas-Jackson, "RAISE IT UP!! Youth Arts and Awareness," *Kalfou* 4, no. 1 (2017): 89–95, http://dx.doi.org/10.15367/kf.v4i1.146.

87. Thomas-Jackson writes that their pedagogy is

rooted in the idea that while marginalized communities are not at fault for the ways in which systems of oppression bear down on, exploit, and subjugate us, we are responsible for liberating ourselves from them. We should not, nor can we afford to, wait for the forces that underwrite our oppression and capitalize from our containment to free us. We know that art helps us to envision the world as it could be, and so we use it as the vehicle to educate and support youth in becoming proactive and radical voices and movers. (Ibid., 90)

CHAPTER THREE. RESTORING
ENVIRONMENTAL JUSTICE

1. In Pellow's conception of critical environmental justice (CEJ), he suggests that "social movements can strategically harness the power of states to produce positive outcomes, but should always be cautious about doing so and work to limit a reliance on the state." David Pellow, "Critical Environmental Justice Studies," in *What Is Critical Environmental Justice?* (Cambridge: Polity, 2017), 151.

2. Nadja Popovich, Livia Albeck-Ripka and Kendra Pierre-Louis, "76 Environmental Rules on the Way Out under Trump," *New York Times,* July 6, 2018, https://www.nytimes.com/interactive/2017/10/05 /climate/trump-environment-rules-reversed.html; Umair Irfan and Christina Amisashaun, "How Trump Is Letting Polluters Off the Hook, in One Chart," *Vox,* June 21, 2018, https://www.vox.com/energy-and-environment/2018/2/22/17036114/pollution-fines-trump-pruitt-epa.

3. "Boots Riley—Bringing Rebellion to the Forefront with 'Sorry to Bother You,'" *The Daily Show with Trevor Noah,* July 16, 2018, YouTube video, 5 min., 7 sec., https://www.youtube.com/watch?v=oc7oiFCaKho.

4. Stepha Velednitsky, "The Case for Ecological Reparations: A Conversation with Jason W. Moore," *Edge Effects,* October 31, 2017, http://edgeeffects.net/jason-w-moore.

5. Society for Ecological Restoration, accessed September 15, 2018, https://www.ser.org.

6. In criminal justice, the notion of restorative justice moves away from punitive models of accountability. It operationalizes the idea that "crime causes harm: justice repairs harm" in a number of different ways. Holly Denning, "Restorative and Environmental Justice Models for Healing Communities in the Wake of Disasters: Hurricane Katrina and Beyond," *Sociological Imagination* 50, no. 1 (2014): 35–55. As Denning describes in her overview of restorative criminal justice, practices such as mediation, community conferencing, and circle dialogues work to "foster empowerment and empathy" (40–41).

7. Sarah M. Conrad, "A Restorative Environmental Justice for Prison E-waste Recycling," *Peace Review* 23, no. 3 (2011): 348–55, https://

doi.org/10.1080/10402659.2011.596071; C. Holly Denning, "Hurricane Katrina, Environmental Racism and Restorative and Community Justice," *VOMA Connections,* no. 23 (Spring 2006), www.voma.org/docs /connect23.pdf. Restoration ecology has some successes (more often in aquatic systems than in human and landscape-focused environments). See Michael L. Rosenzweig, *Win-Win Ecology: How the Earth's Species Can Survive in the Midst of Human Enterprise* (New York: Oxford University Press, 2003).

8. For example, sociologist Kari Norgaard works with the Karuk, environmental policy scholar Beth Rose Middleton works with the Maidu, and Nicholas J. Reo (Chippewa) with the Anishnaabek.

9. Video produced for the SFMOMA event, screened May 2014 (emphasis added), discussed in Julie Sze, "Environmental Justice and Anthropocene Narratives: Recognition and Representation in Kivalina," *Resilience: A Journal of Environmental Humanities* 2, no. 2 (Fall 2015).

10. Survivance is both a "renunciation of dominance, tragedy and victimry" and the continuance of Native stories. Gerald Vizenor, *Manifest Manners: Narratives on Postindian Survivance* (Lincoln: University of Nebraska Press, 1999), vii.

11. Kyle Powys White, "Indigenous Women, Climate Change Impacts, and Collective Action," *Hypatia: A Journal of Feminist Philosophy* 29, no. 3 (2014): 599–616, https://doi.org/10.1111/hypa.12089.

12. Gómez-Barris, *The Extractive Zone,* xv.

13. Living environmentalism rejects the limitations of a narrow-focused politics in favor of a more strategic, relational vision, framed by the Marxist-feminist concept of social reproduction. Giovanna Di Chiro, "Living Environmentalisms: Coalition Politics, Social Reproduction, and Environmental Justice," *Environmental Politics* 17, no. 2 (2008): 276–98, https://doi.org/10.1080/09644010801936230.

14. H. Bruce Franklin, "What Are We to Make of J.G. Ballard's Apocalypse?" 1979, retrievable at www.jgballard.ca/criticism/ballard_ apocalypse_1979.html.

15. Frederic Jameson, "Future City," *New Left Review* 21 (May/ June 2003), https://newleftreview.org/issues/II21/articles/fredric-jameson-future-city.

16. Franklin, "What Are We to Make of J. G. Ballard's Apocalypse?" (emphasis added).

17. Janet Fiskio, "Building Paradise in the Classroom," in *Teaching Climate Change in the Humanities,* ed. Stephen Siperstein, Shane Hall, and Stephanie LeMenager (New York: Routledge, 2017), 101–9.

18. Will Steffen and his fifteen coauthors paint a picture of how a chain of self-reinforcing changes might potentially be initiated. Australian National University, accessed September 15, 2018, http://climate.anu.edu.au/about-us/people/will-steffen.

19. Re-locate Kivalina, accessed October 17, 2018, www.relocate-ak .org.

20. Jen Marlow, quoted in Sze, "Environmental Justice and Anthropocene Narratives."

21. Ibid.

22. P. Joshua Griffin, "Ethics: Translation," *Cultural Anthropology,* April 17, 2013, https://culanth.org/fieldsights/ethics-translation.

23. Fiskio, "Building Paradise in the Classroom," 101 (emphasis added).

24. Ibid., 106.

25. See Robin Kelley's review of his film in "Sorry, Not Sorry," *Boston Review,* September 13, 2018, at http://bostonreview.net/race-literature-culture/robin-d-g-kelley-sorry-not-sorry#.W52dvqFaFDZ.email.

26. Aidan Davison, *Technology and the Contested Meanings of Sustainability* (Albany: State University of New York Press, 2001), 166.

27. Miles Surrey, "WTF: On the Bizarre Ending of 'Sorry to Bother You,'" *Ringer,* July 6, 2018, https://www.theringer.com/movies/2018/7/6/17532550/wtf-on-the-bizarre-ending-of-sorry-to-bother-you.

28. Francesca T. Royster, *Sounding Like a No-No: Queer Sounds and Eccentric Acts in the Post-soul Era* (Ann Arbor: University of Michigan Press, 2013), 30. Royster discusses the rebellious spirit in post–civil rights black music by focusing on a range of offbeat, eccentric, queer, or slippery performances in Eartha Kitt, Stevie Wonder, Grace Jones, P-Funk, and Janelle Monáe.

29. Mark Guarino, "Misleading Reports of Lawlessness after Katrina Worsened Crisis, Officials Say," *Guardian,* August 16, 2015, https://

www.theguardian.com/us-news/2015/aug/16/hurricane-katrina-new-orleans-looting-violence-misleading-reports.

30. Kevin Fox Gotham and Miriam Greenberg, *Crisis Cities: Disaster and Redevelopment in New York and New Orleans* (New York: Oxford University Press, 2014); Kenneth A. Gould and Tammy L. Lewis, *Green Gentrification: Urban Sustainability and the Struggle for Environmental Justice* (New York: Routledge, 2017).

31. Scholars documented this relationship. See Eric Klinenberg, *Heat Wave: A Social Autopsy of Disaster in Chicago* (Chicago: University of Chicago Press, 2002).

32. See "Environmental Justice and Climate Justice Hub" at the Orfalea Center, accessed September 15, 2018, http://ejcj.orfaleacenter .ucsb.edu.

33. Quoted in Scott Shane and Eric Lipton, "Government Saw Flood Risk but Not Levee Failure," *New York Times,* September 2, 2005, https://www.nytimes.com/2005/09/02/us/nationalspecial/government-saw-flood-risk-but-not-levee-failure.html.

34. David Schlosberg, *Defining Environmental Justice: Theories, Movements, and Nature* (New York: Oxford University Press, 2007).

35. Curtis Marez, "What Is a Disaster," *American Quarterly* 61, no. 3 (September 2009): ix–xi.

36. Johari Jabir, "On Conjuring Mahalia: Mahalia Jackson, New Orleans, and the Sanctified Swing," *American Quarterly* 61, no. 3 (September 2009): 649–69, quote on 666.

37. Ibid., 664.

38. Guarino, "Misleading Reports of Lawlessness after Katrina Worsened Crisis."

39. Mike Mariani, "The Tragic, Forgotten History of Zombies," *Atlantic,* October 28, 2015, https://www.theatlantic.com/entertainment /archive/2015/10/how-america-erased-the-tragic-history-of-the-zombie /412264.

40. *Come Hell or High Water: The Battle for Turkey Creek,* directed by Leah Mahan (2013; Zamler Productions, LLC, and the Independent Television Service, 2014), DVD.

41. Claire Jean Kim writes, "The language of conservation has a magical quality. It transforms death into everlasting life. It produces

a heartwarming drama out of a horror story." Claire Jean Kim, "Murder and Mattering in Harambe's House," *Politics and Animals* 3 (2017): 6.

42. Her 2018 documentary *Fear No Gumbo*, along with her album *Queens* (2018), focuses on juvenile justice and lack of "just reconstruction" in the Lower Ninth Ward.

43. Henrick Karoliszyn, "'Trouble the Water' Star 10 Years Later: 'People should never think Katrina is over,'" *Splinter*, August 24, 2015, https://splinternews.com/trouble-the-water-star-10-years-later-people-should-ne-1793850182.

44. In "It Gets Wetter," sociologist Daniel Aldana Cohen writes of two Jesmyn Ward books set in and around De Lisle, Mississippi, as implicitly about climate change. These are *Salvage the Bones* (2011), a novel that unfolds in the days before and during Hurricane Katrina, and *Men We Reaped* (2013), a memoir about the deaths of young black men whom Ward grew up with.

45. Jonathan Lear, *Radical Hope: Ethics in the Face of Cultural Devastation* (Cambridge, MA: Harvard University Press, 2006), 2, 9.

46. Kyle Whyte, "Indigenous Science (Fiction) for the Anthropocene: Ancestral Dystopias and Fantasies of Climate Change Crises," *Environment and Planning E: Nature and Space* 1, nos. 1–2 (2018): 224–42.

47. "Hurricane Statistics Fast Facts," CNN, last modified August 31, 2018, https://www.cnn.com/2013/05/31/world/americas/hurricane-statistics-fast-facts/index.html.

48. "Puerto Rico Rising—#PRontheMap," Vimeo video, 16 min., 55 sec., posted by PR on the Map, November 23, 2017, https://vimeo.com/244218606?ref=fb-share.

49. Umair Irfan, "It's Been More Than 100 Days and Puerto Rico Is Still in the Longest Blackout in US History," *Vox*, January 4, 2018, https://www.vox.com/energy-and-environment/2017/10/30/16560212/puerto-rico-longest-blackout-in-us-history-hurricane-maria-grid-electricity.

50. "Puerto Rico Increases Hurricane Maria Death Toll to 2,975," *BBC News*, August 29, 2018, https://www.bbc.com/news/world-us-canada-45338080.

51. Matthew Yglesias, "Trump's Continued Indolent Response to Hurricane Maria Is Our Worst Fears about Him Come True," *Vox*,

August 29, 2018, https://www.vox.com/2018/8/29/17797466/trump-hurricane-maria-puerto-rico-response-death-toll.

52. During the first nine days after Harvey, FEMA provided 5.1 million meals, 4.5 million liters of water, and more than 20,000 tarps in Houston; in the same amount of time, it delivered, just 1.6 million meals, 2.8 million liters of water, and 5,000 tarps to Puerto Rico. "The U.S. Betrayal of Puerto Rico by the Numbers," *Splinter,* March 27, 2018, https://splinternews.com/ the-u-s-betrayal-of-puerto-rico-by-the-numbers-1824106542.

53. "The Explosion of the Debt Crisis," Puerto Rico Syllabus, accessed September 15, 2018, https://puertoricosyllabus.com/how-the-debt-crisis-exploded.

54. Puerto Rico Syllabus, https://puertoricosyllabus.com; "#Charlestonsyllabus," African American Intellectual History Society, accessed September 15, 2018, https://www.aaihs.org/resources/charlestonsyllabus; NYC Stands with Standing Rock Collective, "#StandingRockSyllabus"; immigration historians affiliated with the Immigration History Research Center at the University of Minnesota and the Immigration and Ethnic History Society, "#ImmigrationSyllabus," last modified January 26, 2017, http://editions.lib.umn.edu/immigrationsyllabus; N.D.B. Connolly and Keisha N. Blain, "Trump Syllabus 2.0," last modified June 28, 2016. www.publicbooks.org/trump-syllabus-2–0; Su'ad Abdul Khabeer, Arshad Ali, Evelyn Alsultany, Sohail Daulatzai, Lara Deeb, Carol Fadda, Zareena Grewal, Juliane Hammer, Nadine Naber, and Junaid Rana, "#IslamophobiaIsRacism Syllabus," Islamophobia Is Racism, accessed September 15, 2018, https://islamophobiaisracism.wordpress.com.

55. "Climate Debt: Making Historical Responsibility Part of the Solution," Friends of the Earth International, December 2005, www.foei.org/en/publications/pdfs/climatedebt.pdf.

56. JunteGente is a coalition that emerged post-Maria with a "people's platform," accessed September 15, 2018, http://juntegente.org. The group is discussed in Oliver Laughland, "'I'm not fatalistic': Naomi Klein on Puerto Rico, Austerity and the Left," *Guardian,* August 8,

2018, https://www.theguardian.com/world/2018/aug/08/naomi-klein-interview-puerto-rico-the-battle-for-paradise?CMP=fb_gu.

57. One group, Resilient Power Puerto Rico, launched just hours after the devastating landfall of Hurricane Maria, with the "goal of bringing power to the most impacted communities through the deployment of solar generation and storage systems." "How It Happens," Resilient Power Puerto Rico, accessed September 15, 2018, https://resilientpowerpr.org/about-us.

58. Ryan Reed, "Lin-Manuel Miranda Details Puerto Rico Arts Fund," *Rolling Stone,* July 23, 2018, https://www.rollingstone.com/culture/culture-news/lin-manuel-miranda-details-puerto-rico-arts-fund-702364; Suzy Exposito, "Lin-Manuel Miranda Talks Puerto Rico Benefit Song 'Almost Like Praying,'" *Rolling Stone,* October 6, 2017, https://www.rollingstone.com/music/music-news/lin-manuel-miranda-talks-puerto-rico-benefit-song-almost-like-praying-129058.

59. "Ave María a Comic Diary of Category 5 Catastrophe" by Rad Rangy, "AVE MARIA—Comic," last modified October 2017, https://www.facebook.com/pg/radrangy/photos/?tab=album&album_id=1433124446765453.

60. George Gene Gustines, "A Puerto Rican Hero Joins with Wonder Woman and Others for Hurricane Relief," *New York Times,* March 20, 2018, https://www.nytimes.com/2018/03/20/books/puerto-rico-hurricane-relief-dc-comics.html.

61. Salil D. Benegal, "The Spillover of Race and Racial Attitudes into Public Opinion about Climate Change," *Environmental Politics* 27, no. 4 (2018): 733–56, https://doi.org/10.1080/09644016.2018.1457287.

62. Marcus Rediker, "You'll Never Be as Radical as This 18th-Century Quaker Dwarf," *New York Times,* August 12, 2017, https://www.nytimes.com/2017/08/12/opinion/sunday/youll-never-be-as-radical-as-this-18th-century-quaker-dwarf.html.

63. Donna Haraway, *Staying with the Trouble: Making Kin in the Chthulucene* (Durham, NC: Duke University Press, 2016), 35.

64. Rediker, "You'll Never Be as Radical as This 18th-Century Quaker Dwarf."

CONCLUSION

Epigraphs: Scott Alden, "UN Scientific Paper Suggests Capitalism Has to Die in Order for the Planet to Be Saved," *Gritpost,* August 28, 2018, https://gritpost.com/un-paper-capitalism; Adrienne Rich, "Credo of a Passionate Skeptic," *Los Angeles Times,* March 11, 2011, retrievable at www.english.illinois.edu/maps/poets/m_r/rich/onlineessays.htm.

1. Pankaj Mirsa, "The Religion of Whiteness Becomes a Suicide Cult," *New York Times,* August 30, 2018, https://www.nytimes.com/2018/08/30/opinion/race-politics-whiteness.html.

2. Kelley, "Sorry, Not Sorry."

3. Junot Diaz, "Under President Trump, Radical Hope Is Our Best Weapon," *New Yorker,* November 21, 2016, https://www.newyorker.com/magazine/2016/11/21/under-president-trump-radical-hope-is-our-best-weapon; Carolina De Robertis, ed., *Radical Hope: Letters of Love and Dissent in Dangerous Times* (New York: Vintage, 2017); Lear, *Radical Hope.*

4. Interview with Antoine Dangerfield, "We Rise Together Homie," *Jacobin,* August 3, 2018. https://jacobinmag.com/2018/08/wildcat-strike-indianapolis-shut-down.

5. Doreen St. Félix, "The Otherworldly Concept Albums of Janelle Monae," *New Yorker,* March 1, 2018, https://www.newyorker.com/culture/culture-desk/the-otherworldly-concept-albums-of-janelle-monae; Elsa First, "The Secret Life of Plants," *New York Times,* December 30, 1973, https://www.nytimes.com/1973/12/30/archives/the-secret-life-of-plants-by-peter-tompkins-and-christopher-bird.html; Tristin Wang, "The Secret Life of Plants," *Harvard Science Review,* January 22, 2014, https://harvardsciencereview.com/2014/01/22/the-secret-life-of-plants.

6. Royster, *Sounding Like a No-No,* 87. *Quare* means "the performance of 'excess' or outsiderhood from the already marginalized cultural boundaries of the black community" (14).

7. Ella Davies, "Barnacle Gosling's Terrifying Cliff Tumble," *BBC Earth,* October 17, 2014, www.bbc.com/earth/story/20141020-chicks-tumble-of-terror-filmed; Susan Casey, "The Orca, Her Dead Calf and Us," *New York Times,* August, 4, 2018, https://www.nytimes.com/2018/08/04/opinion/sunday/the-orca-her-dead-calf-and-us.html.

8. Kelley, "Sorry, Not Sorry."

GLOSSARY

ANTI-CAPITALISM A broad set of beliefs and policies that range from taming the worst excesses of capitalism to radically reimagining the fundamental tenets of how economies function and are organized, such as in socialism.

CLIMATE JUSTICE A global movement for justice in addressing the historical dimensions, current policies (or lack of) regarding sea-level rise, ocean acidification, increasing intensities related to drought and wildfires, etc., and future implications of massive carbon emissions and their interrelated impacts on ecological systems and human communities.

DISPOSSESSION A term most often used in relation to the process of settler colonial expansion or the movement of Native peoples from their ancestral lands. Dispossession also applies in broader contexts, such as in urban displacement and gentrification.

ENVIRONMENTAL JUSTICE (EJ) A social movement to further policy and cultural changes that support social justice and environmentalism, broadly defined, connecting issues of race, class, indigeneity, gender, citizenship/nation-state, and sexuality with environmental equity.

EXTRACTION The unsustainable use of natural resources (oil, mining, etc.), often shaped by race/racism and colonial histories/neocolonial policies.

GENDERED ENVIRONMENTAL VIOLENCE The both visible and invisible ways in which environmental changes or policies have a gendered component.

INTERSECTIONALITY A framework in which axes of identity and difference, such as race, gender, sexuality, national origin, and ability/disability, are interconnected. The concept emerged out of black feminist thought.

LIBERALISM Historically, a set of universalist beliefs that prioritize the individual and freedom, particularly the freedom to own property. Under liberalism, individuals are free to safeguard themselves and their property from the excesses of the state.

NEOLIBERALISM A set of policies and worldviews that favors private markets and corporate power. Elements of neoliberal policy include tax cuts, privatization of public services, and deregulation.

RACIAL CAPITALISM The argument that capitalism and racism depended on one another as coevolving philosophical, political, and economic systems during the transition from Western feudal societies to modernity, which relied on colonialism, slavery, violence, and genocide.

SETTLER COLONIALISM A system that was and remains a particular form of colonialism in which Indigenous inhabitants of a specific place were and are replaced by settlers. Settler colonialism is both historical and ongoing as well as cultural and political in its character and practices.

SLOW VIOLENCE The idea that violence has a temporal character, which manifests how the impacts of violence are often rendered invisible for those impacted by it, as well as made difficult to see for those not directly impacted. These impacts often take a long period of time, in contrast to fast violence, which is sudden, obvious, and explosive.

SOLIDARITY The sense of community or group connection around a set of shared values. Solidarity is most often manifested through labor politics, social movements, and cultural expression.

SELECTED BIBLIOGRAPHY

Estes, Nick. *Our History Is the Future: Standing Rock versus the Dakota Access Pipeline, and the Long Tradition of Indigenous Resistance*. New York: Verso, 2019.

Estes, Nick, and Jaskiran Dhillon, eds. *Standing with Standing Rock: Voices from the #NoDAPL Movement*. Minneapolis: University of Minnesota, 2019.

Gilmore, Ruth Wilson. *Golden Gulag: Prisons, Surplus, Crisis, and Opposition in Globalizing California*. Berkeley: University of California Press, 2007.

Gómez-Barris, Macarena. *The Extractive Zone: Social Ecologies and Decolonial Perspectives*. Durham, NC: Duke University Press, 2017.

Hoover, Elizabeth. *The River Is in Us: Fighting Toxics in a Mohawk Community*. Minneapolis: University of Minnesota Press, 2017.

Kelley, Robin D. G. *Freedom Dreams: The Black Radical Imagination*. Boston: Beacon Press, 2002.

Klein, Naomi. *The Battle for Paradise: Puerto Rico Takes On the Disaster Capitalists*. Chicago: Haymarket Books, 2018.

Pauli, Benjamin. *Flint Fights Back: Environmental Justice and Democracy in the Flint Water Crisis*. Cambridge, MA: MIT Press, 2019.

Pellow, David Naguib. *What Is Critical Environmental Justice?* Cambridge: Polity, 2017.

Sze, Julie, ed. *Sustainability: Approaches to Environmental Justice and Social Power.* New York: New York University Press, 2018.

Voyles, Traci Brynne. *Wastelanding: Legacies of Uranium Mining in Navajo Country.* Minneapolis: University of Minnesota Press, 2015.

Founded in 1893,
UNIVERSITY OF CALIFORNIA PRESS
publishes bold, progressive books and journals
on topics in the arts, humanities, social sciences,
and natural sciences—with a focus on social
justice issues—that inspire thought and action
among readers worldwide.

The UC PRESS FOUNDATION
raises funds to uphold the press's vital role
as an independent, nonprofit publisher, and
receives philanthropic support from a wide
range of individuals and institutions—and from
committed readers like you. To learn more, visit
ucpress.edu/supportus.

CPSIA information can be obtained
at www.ICGtesting.com
Printed in the USA
LVHW011605081219
639822LV00002B/383/P